JAMES C.
SHEPPARD, M. D.

"It Was the Right Thing to Do."

JAMES C. SHEPPARD, M. D.

"It Was the Right Thing to Do."

A Biography
By
Sam Carnley

James C. Sheppard, M. D.
© 2022 Sam Carnley & Dr. James C. Sheppard

Library of Congress Catalog Card Number:
ISBN: 978-1-4583-5043-5
Imprint: Lulu.com

Published by:
Lulu Press, Inc.
P. O. Box 12018
Durham, NC 27709

Cover: created and designed by the author consisting of the elements described below:

Front cover panel photo collage elements include Dr. Sheppard's "Big Barn," in the back ground and his rare 1925 C. L. Best 60 Logging Cruiser in the foreground.

Back cover panel photo depicts restored vintage tractors housed in Dr. Sheppard's "Big Barn." All tractor photos made and copyrighted by the author.

Dedicated first, to my dear wife, Nell, for putting up
with the many hours and days I spent interviewing
Dr. Sheppard and sitting at the computer writing
this, my first book and second, to the late Mrs.
Velma Teal Mathis, my Paxton High School
English teacher who inspired my writing in high
school and beyond.

CONTENTS

PHOTO LISTS

Miscellaneous Photos

Wheel Tractor Photos

Crawler Tractor Photos

≈ACKNOWLEDGEMENTS≈

I am deeply grateful to Dr. Jimmy Sheppard for entrusting me to author the telling of his life story as my first book. His children, Penny, Pam and Ballard are also due many thanks for their invaluable contributions in making the story complete as it relates to their roles in the family as well.

Sam Carnley

I

≈REHOBETH≈

From Birth to High School Graduation.

There lies along the banks of historic Bruce Creek meandering through Panhandle Florida's Walton County one hundred and sixty acres of unspoiled natural beauty owned by retired M. D., Dr. James Sheppard.

On the property once stood the village of the Sam Story band of Euchee Indians who welcomed the County's first white settlers and for whom Euchee Valley where the land is situated was named.

At first glance, the scenery appears unblemished by man-made intrusions, but on closer inspection, the outlines of a massive house and several large barns topped in silver-grey corrugated roofing metal come into focus on the fringes of the woods skirting a large open meadow of several dozen acres.

The weathered grey of the building walls planked in cypress mutes their outlines, softly blending them into the natural surroundings.

There is nothing natural though, about the contents of the barns, for they house some one hundred and sixty classic tractors the eighty-seven-year-old Doctor has restored to like new condition over decades of collecting them. Consisting primarily of John Deere farm tractors, they also include 50 Caterpillar crawlers and a sprinkling of Cletracs as well as a few others.

His love of tractors, especially the colorful green and yellow John Deere, began on the farm where he grew up between Rehobeth and Taylor below Dothan in south Alabama's Houston County. He and his parents moved there after having lived on two other farms previously.

At the time of Jimmy's birth on 13 December 1934, his parents, Arthur and Lola Clyde Kornegay Sheppard, lived in the home of his mother's parents. The oldest of three children, the name on his birth certificate is Jimmy Clyde Sheppard with a middle name shared by his mother and Dr. Irby Clyde Bates who delivered him at home.

Jimmy is who he always has been and remains to most acquaintances, but while working his way through college toward his medical degree, he found that because those entering his name in their records assumed his first name to be James, it had become his official identity even though not in agreement with his birth certificate.

Worrying that the discrepancy between the records might lead to future identification issues, he engaged a local attorney to petition the court to declare James C. Sheppard as a second legal name by which he was also known as, to which the court agreed in a decree issued to that effect.

Such concerns however, remained many years ahead of Jimmy when, at about age 2 and a half his conscious life began with a large white oak basket as his first memory. It sat under a shade tree at the end of a cotton field and his mother placed him in it for safe keeping while she picked cotton.

The field belonged to Ide Harrell for whom his daddy share cropped when Jimmy was born. His mother worked in the fields too and the basket passed as her babysitter. She placed a quilt pallet in the bottom to lay him on and gave him a bottle.

The basket sat where she could see it from anywhere in the field and she checked on him from time to time to keep him safe and comfortable.

His parents lived on the little they made as tenants growing cotton and peanuts in the field next to old man Harrell's house. On that particular day when he first became aware of his surroundings, Jimmy got the idea he might just turn that basket over and get out. He had seen Ide Harrell drive his car up to the house and park it in the barn.

After tipping the basket over and crawling out, he struck out across the field along the fence row to the barn and finding the door unfastened, went inside. It seemed so novel to him that he opened the car door and climbing up in the seat, began honking the horn.

When it continued longer than seemed normal, Arthur and Lola who could hear it thought old man Harrell might be signaling for help in some sort of an emergency so Arthur dashed over to see. It surprised him on entering the barn to find his little son the perpetrator of the racket.

It came as no less of a surprise to Jimmy when his daddy suddenly appeared and asked him, "what are you doing in this car?" The words fell so profoundly on Jimmy's ears as to leave them as his second most vivid memory of that day.

He less fondly remembered Arthur pulling him out of the car and marching him crying back to the cotton patch with the encouragement of a keen peach tree switch.

Most parents then still believed in the "spare not the rod; spoil not the child" proverb. Whipping Jimmy at that age, Arthur believed, would teach him it is wrong to invade the privacy and property of others. Arthur had never whipped his son before, and rarely ever did so again.

During their time on the Ide Harrell farm Jimmy played with the old man's grandchildren, Catherine and John. At 6 and 8 years of age they became his steadfast companions even though at his age they saw him as little more than a toddler.

He tagged along when they went swimming and fishing in the creek behind the house. They had fishing poles but he didn't so they improvised him one using number 8 sewing thread for a line, a bent straight pin for a hook and a long slender branch broken off a tree limb for a pole.

Lacking an eye in the pin for threading the line through, they instead knotted it firmly around the pin beneath its head, which worked just as well. He fished like they did but never caught anything because the hook had no barb to hold the fish and they easily slipped free.

After escaping from the cotton basket and hearing his daddy's words, his next earliest memories were of fishing with Ide Harrell's grandchildren. His parents worked the Harrell farm until about Jimmy's third year.

They then went to live with a great Aunt Jenny whose husband died suddenly leaving her and three children in need of someone to run the farm. They remained there about a year and in addition to working the farm, Arthur ran the Rehobeth cotton gin during the harvest season.

He worked as head ginner, a position he won in a contest with 2 other men. Each contestant ginned 3 bales of cotton. Arthur got the job because he knew better than the others how to set the gin heads so they stripped the most lint from the seeds thereby yielding the greatest weight per bale.

He could also detect problems with the gin by the sounds it made. On one occasion he noticed the usual dull roar of the machinery begin to rise in pitch and knew immediately the steam engine governor had failed. He sprinted from the gin house to the steam engine in another building and shut it down.

His fast action saved the engine from self-destructing as it rose to a speed above which it was designed to run. His job at the gin stretched from 6 in the morning to 6 in the evening, 6 days a week.

With no transportation other than his feet, he walked the mile between the gin and Aunt Jenny's house which stood at the end of a long lane. Jimmy recalled sitting in the swing on her back porch watching for Arthur to come walking down the lane when he knocked off in the evenings.

After their stay at the Aunt Jenny farm the Sheppards moved again to a 43-acre farm owned by Jim Jones, a Dothan business man. He bought it from Arthur's great uncle, Henry Brown, who had moved to Freeport, Florida. Jones invited them to live on the farm as tenants, which they did for a time but eventually bought it and Jimmy grew up there.

It originally began as a rough, unpainted wood frame tenant shack with a single large room. Later "lean to" additions made before the Sheppards moved in included a kitchen on the back, or north side, a small room on the east side and a porch and another small room on the south side, into which the front door opened.

Beneath the shade of a pecan tree here and there, it sat in an unfenced yard of white sand void of grass. They swept it with a yard broom to keep it clean and free of grass as a deterrent to fire.

Adjacent to the front yard a primitive 2 trail road ran east and west, connecting at each end on more substantial roads running north and south. Years after Jimmy grew up and left home, the county named it Arthur Sheppard Road, and later still, paved it.

With no electricity or indoor plumbing, kerosene lamps lit the house by night and an outhouse served in the absence of one inside. The first female of the house enjoyed the convenience of slop jars or chamber pots overnight and the males relieved their bladders in the back yard and dashed to the outhouse in the dark for more urgent business.

Recycled Sears and Roebuck catalogs and corn cobs met their toilet paper needs.

They drew their water in a gray galvanized 2-gallon bucket on the end of a long rope they dropped down an open well a few yards up slope from the house in an adjoining field.

A fireplace in the living room and a wood stove in the kitchen warmed them in winter. On hot summer nights doors and windows stood open as outlets for the stifling temperature built up in the house during the heat of the day. Otherwise, they had little to cool themselves beyond their sweat.

That of the brow ruled their waking hours as another proverb they lived by, not only in the fields but in most everything they did. Jimmy's many chores included feeding and watering the livestock.

Toting water to the mules and cows required walking with a 2-gallon bucket of water in each hand from the well on the north side of the house to their stalls next to the barn west of the house.

Walking between them took not just a few steps, but hundreds, with the heavy buckets straining his shoulders and arms. Making several such round trips in one watering could prove quite exhausting. The task required repeating 7 days a week year in and year out.

Hand washing their clothes similarly consumed much water and labor. Every Monday morning Jimmy and Lola filled a trio of number 3 galvanized wash tubs of about 15 gallons each, and a wash pot of only a few gallons less.

That required drawing from the well, in buckets of 2 gallons at the time, more than 25 pails of water for a single washing.

After filling the soot blackened cast iron pot, they lit a fire under it. When it boiled, they put the clothes in and stirred them with a batter stick to loosen soiling. Then lifting them from the hot water on the stick like spaghetti hanging on a fork they laid them on a wood block cut from a large tree trunk and beat them with the stick.

That helped remove soiling in the same way a washing machine agitator would. Following that they dipped every article of clothing once in each of the 3 tubs of rinse water and hung them dripping wet on the line. This ritual followed a weekly routine taking the better part of a day.

Arthur continued farming with the mules on the new place the same as he had done previously with peanuts and cotton as his cash crops. And as in the past, Jimmy continued going to the fields with his parents but his days of sitting in the basket were over.

By about age 4 he joined his parents as they inched along the seemingly endless rows on their knees or stood with stooped backs meticulously plucking the snowy white tufts from the bolls and stuffing them into their pick sacks.

He came to appreciate at that young age the hostility of a cotton patch long since known to his parents. The sweltering dog-days heat conspired with the cotton plant against the theft of its progeny in exacting a toll on pickers.

After millennia of cultivation, the plant had learned the optimal height of growth most confounding to those who would rob it of the ability to reproduce by taking away it's seeds which are the essence of cotton.

It stood at the precise point above the ground rendering uninterrupted comfort in picking neither from bended knee nor arched back, but at some point in between unattainable by humans except in the absence of gravity.

It seems ridiculous to suggest that plants learn, even though nature sometimes moves in ways analogous to conscious thought. But the existence of malice in nature can't be denied.

How else can thorns, cacti, toxic leaves and fruits, insect eating plants, poison ivy, biting and stinging insects, venomous snakes and the like be explained. These are all intended to inflict harm, which is the definition of malice.

Whether malice on the part of cotton played a role in the pain inflicted on pickers mattered little, because the outcome remained the same.

They still ended up with painful knees, aching backs and fingers pricked raw by the needle-sharp points of dried cotton boll bracts.

After enduring all those abuses, not to mention tormenting gnats swarming about the face and crawling in eyes, ears and nose, a day in the cotton patch often ended in exhaustion with little accomplished. Pickers typically received 2 cents a pound, which amounted to only 2 dollars per 100 pounds picked.

That consisted of their earnings for a day's work from sun up to sun down. Many pickers earned even less because not everybody could pick a hundred pounds of cotton in a day.

As a 4-year-old, Jimmy certainly could not, but dragging his own child size pick sack his mother made for him strapped across his shoulder he took the work just as seriously as his parents. With many more years in the cotton field to come, he would do more than his share of picking before moving on beyond that phase of his life.

As he grew older his parents gave him no more duties than he could handle. They required no work of him at the expense of his schooling because with only a 5th grade education themselves, they were learning the harsh lesson of how poorly prepared they were in making a decent living in spite of their hard work.

They wanted their children to have a better future than they did. The intelligence and resourcefulness they displayed in making a living under difficult circumstances on the other hand revealed them as highly functional individuals regardless of their limited formal education.

As a healthy and hard-working couple, neither ever showed an inclination of expecting the other to carry more than an equal share of the work. Arthur stood about 5 feet, 8 inches tall, with a medium build and brown hair and eyes.

Never overweight, he typically dressed in Big Mac blue denim overalls, long sleeve shirt and brogan shoes. In the winter he might wear a coat if cold enough outside and he seldom exited the house bare of his dirt brown fedora.

By nature, a kind, gentle and compassionate man, he never tired of doing people favors, unlike Lola who had a short fuse and sometimes let her mouth lead her astray. The only time Jimmy remembered them being at odds came when she spoke to Arthur in a way she shouldn't have.

He came in from working in the field to find her angry because his brother had stopped by and left an old used ice box on their porch. Venting her displeasure on Arthur, she wanted to know why the son of a bitch dumped his junk on their place for white folks that couldn't afford anything.

Hearing her say those words about his brother angered Arthur beyond the limits of what his normally gentle nature would tolerate. The words had barely left her lips before Arthur back handed her across the face so hard, she went sprawling into a nearby rocking chair.

More resilient than her small 5-foot 2-inch frame would lead anyone to believe, she suffered no serious physical injuries in the encounter which Jimmy witnessed at the tender age of 4. Emotionally and psychologically though, it altered her relationship with her husband for the rest of her life in that she discussed all future differences with him civilly.

Later explaining why his brother left the ice box, Arthur told her that as game warden of the Army base at Fort Benning, Georgia, someone gave him a kerosene fueled refrigerator in replacement of the ice box.

No longer having any use for it, he offered it to Arthur telling him he would bring it by the next time he visited the neighborhood. Arthur made the mistake of neglecting to tell Lola about it ahead of time.

Lola may have learned to keep her temper in check with her husband but not with errant children. She would get on Jimmy's case with little provocation and give him a taste of the razor strop she kept close at hand for putting him back in line.

As the disciplinarian in the family, she recognized the difference between judicious corporal punishment and child abuse and never allowed her temper to push her across the line into the more dangerous of the two. She tolerated no disobedience or back talk.

Jimmy admitted he inherited enough of her temperament that he sometimes behaved in ways putting them at odds, but learned pretty quickly pushing back too hard made things worse for him. He learned he had best go ahead and do what she wanted.

Later in life she told him she regretted whipping him as often as she did, but she didn't know any other way of dealing with how he sometimes behaved. Jimmy found early on that he could negotiate with his more easy-going dad, but not with her because it was her way or no way.

As did most people, both Arthur and Lola indulged in an unhealthy habit or two. He chewed tobacco and smoked but cigarettes never became something he couldn't do without.

He smoked no more than half a dozen a day and quit in his late 40s. He grew his tobacco for chewing in the garden. After harvesting it he had his own tricks of the trade for curing, sweetening and pressing it into the final product.

Lola, known to family and friends as "Shoodie," dipped snuff most of her life but in a very modest way. She did it so rarely and discreetly that few people knew it and a little can of Rooster Snuff lasted her several weeks. Her parents were Robert P. and Rese Hughes Kornegay.

She and Arthur lived with them at the time of Jimmy's birth. They lived then on the old Moats place, so named for the family who previously owned it. Lola's mother died about 4 years after Jimmy's birth. Her father, once fairly prosperous, owned 6 hundred acres of land. He became an alcoholic and the older he got the more he drank.

Due to that he finally lost all his land and died in poverty after literally drinking himself to death. He lived with Arthur and Lola the last few years of his life during which he suffered from Alzheimers, unaware of who he was. While with them he remained alcohol free because they denied him access to it.

He died in 1940 when they lived on the Jim Jones farm and in 1941 Jimmy at age 6 entered the 1st grade at Rehobeth School about 2 miles from the farm and from where he would graduate 12 years later.

For the first couple of years, he rode the bus because his parents preferred that to his walking the 4-mile round trip to school and back at his young age. But from the third grade until age 16 he walked.

He struggled in his first year of school, to the point of almost flunking. His teacher denied knowing why, but as he explained it, he had no idea what the teacher expected of him because he had no recollection of her ever telling him.

Something he did recollect about that year was the bully in his class who took him behind the school house every day at recess and beat him up. But that lasted only until he learned to fight back.

Figuring out he needed to get in the first lick before taking one himself, the next time the boy started pushing him around, Jimmy put his fist squarely in his nose, bloodying it. The sight of his own blood scared the boy, at which point he started crying and ran. That broke him from picking on Jimmy.

He solved his bullying problem, but his marks needed improvement as he headed into second grade. His most vivid memory of that school term had more to do with an event at recess one day than with his academic record.

He and a group of classmates wandered over to the new brick high school building site. They played train by walking single file holding onto the overall galluses of the person in front of each other.

As they came chugging train-like out of a pit at the rear of the site where the foundation had been dug their teacher, Mrs. Ethel Underwood, saw them. Knowing they were not supposed to be there she went over and herded them to the classroom.

In disciplining them, she said "didn't I tell you not to go over there," to which they replied "yes ma'am." "Well, what were you doing over there," she asked. "Playing," they said. "Well, why were you playing over there when I told you not to," she scolded. Not knowing what else to say in their defense, they offered nothing further.

The conversation over, she picked up her paddle to administer punishment. Playing along with their train analogy, she told them, "Well, I am going to fire your train so you won't go back over there." With a round of paddling sparing no one, she made her point.

As he did then and would do in the future, Jimmy told his parents about his punishment and the reasons for it. Repeating the teacher's words, he told them "Just like she said, she fired our train."

His quoting what the teacher said tickled Arthur. He said "she took care of that so I don't have to go back over there," implying he saw hearing the teacher's version as unnecessary in getting the story straight. "Yes sir," Jimmy said.

Although 2nd grade ended in a lackluster performance, he came out of his doldrums going into the 3rd with much improved marks on his report card. His grasp of subject matter gelled, setting him on a course of superb academic performance culminating in his recognition as an honor student for the remainder of elementary through high school and graduation.

His success in school tended to belie the excuse of modern day liberal educational apologists that impoverished children who perform poorly in school do so because of the low socioeconomic status of their families.

They make that claim as justification for all manner of federal and state programs purportedly aimed at reducing poverty as an impediment to a child's ability to perform at grade level in school.

But after generations of wasting untold sums of tax payer dollars on those programs, millions of poor children perform even worse in school now than they did back then.

If being poor dooms children to life-long failure, then Jimmy and millions of his peers growing up under similar conditions in the southern United States should have had no expectation of ever succeeding in life. He would go on however, to defy any such expectations.

The first of the two houses he lived in when growing up originally had no electricity and never indoor plumbing. That fact alone would have qualified him as impoverished in today's world, entitling him and his family to an array of government benefits both at home and at school.

The apologists are at a loss however to explain why children receiving those benefits today are still failing miserably while Jimmy who grew up to succeed beyond the average person's wildest dreams did so without them.

In his early life, Jimmy's family did without many things, among them, an automobile. A 2-mule wagon took them wherever they needed to go although considerably slower than a motor vehicle, which limited their trips to Dothan to about once a year. They went in the fall before school began, mainly to buy Jimmy's Big Mac overalls and shoes.

In addition to clothing, they bought supplies he would need for the coming school term. They also took the once-a-year opportunity to buy other things they needed, such as clothes for Arthur and Lola that she couldn't sew and sundry other items they needed before their next annual trek to town.

With the shorter days at that time of the year squeezing the 20-mile round trip at a mule's pace in between dawn and dusk proved quite an accomplishment if they could do it.

Making the trips quicker would require pushing the mules at an abusive pace which they chose not to do.

If they wanted to spare the mules and go places faster at the same time, they needed an automobile. Arthur had long realized that but never got around to buying one until shortly before Jimmy entered the first grade.

Although President Franklin D. Roosevelt signed the law creating the Rural Electrification Administration, or REA, in 1935, it would take more than 10 years for it to bring electricity to the Rehobeth community.

In the absence of electric powered refrigeration needed to make ice, if residents of the area wanted any, they had to travel 10 miles to Dothan and buy it from the ice plant. Arthur saw in that situation an opportunity for making a few extra dollars in addition to his farm income and Lola's brother, Jay, would play a role in making it happen.

Jay, the most prosperous of Lola's siblings, ran a headstone and vault business at Flomaton in west Alabama close to Jay, Florida. Well enough off to afford it, he bought a new car every year or so.

In 1938 he bought a new 4 door Buick and drove it over to the Sheppard's farm on a visit. Due to heavy rain, the little stream normally only a few inches deep that crossed the road near the farm had swollen to a greater depth.

Thinking he could ford the stream as he had done many times before, Jay drove his new Buick into it. Much to his surprise, the car stalled and water flowed in the windows on one side and out those on the other.

Arthur pulled it out with his mules, but Jay told him the water ruined the car and he would have to junk it. Undaunted by its loss, Jay went and bought another new one.

Jay also owned a 1938 stake bed Chevrolet pickup he no longer needed due to it being too small to handle the heavy stuff he hauled in his business, so, he let Arthur have it for a very low price he would have sold it to no one else for.

A fairly new truck when Arthur bought it in 1939 or 40, he had the idea of using it for a delivery route selling ice to residents of the Rehobeth area who had no ready access to it otherwise. Several times a week, he drove to the ice plant in Dothan and loaded the truck with 300-pound blocks of ice.

The vehicle's load capacity limited how much he could haul, which consisted of about 6 blocks weighing in total just short of a ton. He covered it with a tarpaulin to reduce melting and keep it free of dust from the dirt roads he traveled over.

On Mondays, Wednesdays and Fridays he ran one route and on Tuesdays Thursdays and Saturdays he ran another. He alternated between them on a schedule timed to bring ice to customers on each route about every other day, that being about how long the previous delivery lasted them.

Using an ice pick, he chipped from the big blocks smaller ones in sizes he estimated as equal to what the customer ordered. He then took it into the house with his ice tongs and placed it in their ice box.

He ran the ice routes during slack times on the farm and in the summers when Jimmy had no school, he took him along on the deliveries. Any time a customer wanted a small piece of ice, like a nickel or dime's worth, he let Jimmy take it in with the tongs and put it in the customer's ice box.

Seeing Jimmy do that, country people who made up the majority of Arthur's customers, called him smart, not as to his intelligence, but his industriousness in working with his daddy at such a young age.

For that reason, they treated him with cookies and other goodies. He liked doing it for the treats, but he also enjoyed spending the time with his dad because they were best friends. On a typical day they left for town at 4 in the morning, stopped for breakfast 30 minutes later and then arrived at the ice plant when it opened at 5:00 to load the truck with ice.

One morning while enjoying their usual breakfast of grits, eggs and ham, Jimmy noticed on the counter a beautiful chocolate cake under a glass cover. After they finished and were leaving, he asked his dad why they had the cake under the glass.

Arthur said it's beautiful and stimulates people's appetites, but it's not made to eat, it's just made to sell. Jimmy thought about it a while and then asked if people that buy it eat it, and Arthur said of course they do but most people can't afford it. Jimmy took that to mean eating it a luxury not shared by those unable to buy it.

Sharing that particular pleasure may have been beyond their means, but others were not. As an avid fisherman, Arthur always found time for the pleasure of dunking a fishing hook in his favorite stream or pond, of which the area had no shortage. He began taking Jimmy along on the fishing trips at a very young age.

On one of the earliest trips, Jimmy remembered catfishing on a creek about 3 miles from their farm. It ran across the back side of a farm owned by the family of Jimmy's friend and school mate, Foster Watkins. When they took a notion to go fishing, Jimmy and Arthur would knock off work in the late afternoon, an hour or so before dusk.

They took a bag containing their fishing lines and hooks, a frying pan, some cooking oil, a quilt for sleeping on and a little meal and flour and headed down to the creek. When they got there, they rigged up a dozen or more hooks and lines.

For poles, they cut long slender stalks from brush growing along the creek, stripped off the branches and leaves and tied their lines to the ends with the smallest tips.

Sharpening the butt ends, they pushed each pole into the soft earth of the creek bank deep enough to hold them securely against the struggles of the biggest fish they would likely catch.

They spaced out the poles along a quarter mile stretch of the bank. On the return trip to the spot where they had put down their quilt for camping, they baited the hooks with whatever bait they had brought along and flipped the lines out into the creek.

Jimmy, aged 4 or 5 at the time, tagged a little behind Arthur who decided to cross the creek over a fallen log and plant some poles on the other side of the stream.

When Jimmy saw Arthur headed for the opposite side, he hurried to catch up. At the end of the log on his side of the creek, a mass of drift wood and trash had piled up against it. In his haste, he thought he could take a short cut across the trash to get onto the log quicker.

To his surprise, when he stepped onto it, he splashed through into the water. Arthur stood on the far end of the log waiting for Jimmy to catch up. When he saw him go into the water he crossed back over the log, reached down, fished him out by his galluses and stood him on the log soaking wet.

Arthur asked him why he tried to cross the debris and Jimmy replied that it looked like trash he could walk on. "Yeah," Arthur told him, "It was trash, but water was underneath it."

They continued working the catfish poles until about midnight. Without flashlights or lanterns to see in the dark, they lit their way along the creek unhooking their catches and re-baiting their hooks in the glow of flaming "lighterd knot" torches.

The resin impregnated knots were all that remained of the plentiful stands of long-leaf yellow pines that once towered over the country side.

Igniting easily and burning with an unforgettable aromatic scent, they picked up off the ground enough of the knots to fuel an all-night fire in hardly any time at all.

With the skillet and cooking supplies they brought, they fried their supper from the first of their catch. Even though they always brought a quilt along, they did not spend the night every time. Those times they didn't, they hiked the 3 miles home in the dark.

Their reasons for staying or not, varied. If the fish bit well, for instance, they might stay. If they did not, they might quit early and go home to sleep in their beds, hoping for better luck the next time out.

Not far from their farm a small wet-weather pond had formed in a low spot that held water year-round as long as sufficient rain fell to keep it filled. About the year Jimmy turned 6, it started going dry for the first time in 10 or so years.

A neighbor stopped by and told Arthur about it, saying it probably had fish in it after that many years and they were just going to die when it completely dried up. They decided to go to the pond and if they found any fish in it, they would bring them home.

Taking their hoes along, they used them to muddy the water which remained only a few inches deep. The muddying depleted the oxygen, causing the fish to float to the surface where they could be picked up and put in a bucket. Jimmy went along happily gathering up fish until he grabbed what he thought to be a really big one.

As he pulled it out of the water it seemed to grow longer the higher he lifted it and he suddenly realized he held a cotton mouth moccasin in his hands. It squirmed and twisted about, trying to bite him, but the tall grass he stood in prevented it from doing so and he dropped it faster than he had picked it up.

That ended his fishing for the day but it took him years to live down the kidding about mistaking a snake for a fish.

On another occasion, his dad took him fishing on Spring Creek in southeast Houston County near the state line with Jackson County, Florida.

He remembered that trip not so much for the fishing, but for the scare an angry mama alligator gave him in the creek. Clad in his overalls and long-sleeve shirt, he sat cross-legged and bare-foot in a wash tub lodged in the black rubber dough nut of a car tire inner tube. As the current swept him along in his makeshift boat, he saw several baby alligators doing something peculiar.

The tiny reptiles measuring about 7 inches long, climbed up a log sticking out of the water at an angle, and leaped back into the creek, which they kept doing repeatedly as if playing.

Steering himself over to the log with the stubby cedar board serving as his paddle, he reached out and picked up one of the babies and laid it in the bottom of his tub. It immediately began grunting a distress call, signaling its mother for help. And mother responded instantaneously.

Jimmy realized he had committed a "no-no" when the creek suddenly erupted in the most turbulent and uproarious splashing, churning and muddying of the water imaginable.

Frightened by the sudden ruckus of the irate mama gator violently thrashing the water, he paddled madly for dry land. The instant his tube boat touched the nearest sand bar, he grabbed the baby gator, leapt out and raced for what he feared to be his life in search of Arthur.

He ran a half a mile across the mud flats leading away from the creek, frantically weaving and dodging and leaping to avoid bog holes in his path, fearing if he landed in one, he would sink to his waist and surely become gator bait.

He swore he heard the gator pursuing him, but dreading what he might see if he looked back, he kept his eyes straight ahead. After a bit the pursuing sounds faded and he felt himself no longer in danger. A glance back revealed no gator in sight except the tiny one he clutched in his hand, still grunting.

When he caught up to his dad out of breath and covered in mud, Arthur asked him what happened. On hearing the story, he laughed, telling him he should have just dropped the grunting baby to end the chase. "I did not think of that," Jimmy told him.

He took the baby gator home to become another of his many pets. He raised it until it grew to about 3 feet long. At that point it had out grown the wash tub Jimmy kept it in and his mother persuaded him to take it to the creek and release it.

Another time in the same creek, he caught a "red breasted" bream. He thought it the prettiest fish he had ever seen and wanted to save it. Taking it home to show his parents, he kept it alive in a bucket of water for a few days.

He knew he could not keep it in the pail indefinitely, but neither did he want to take it back to the creek because he wanted it closer by.

In trying to think of the nearest place with water where it would survive, the well came to mind. Suspecting his parents might object to the well having a fish in it, he surreptitiously carried the bucket of water holding the fish to the well and poured it, fish and all, into the well bucket. He lowered it down on the rope and let the bucket submerge so the fish could swim out.

Days, then weeks and months passed, and no one said anything about a fish in the well. Every day or two, Jimmy peered down the well shaft and could see the fish swimming around.

Then one day, Lola came into the house and in a tone meaning trouble, said "Jimmy, what did you do with that red breasted bream you brought to the house?" Fearing she had discovered his secret, he feigned ignorance. "What do you mean Mom?" he replied.

Even more emphatically than before, she said "I mean what did you do with that red breasted bream you brought to the house?" Scrambling mentally for an answer least likely to further enflame her ire, he knew she felt great sympathy for the plight of innocent animals, so, he framed his answer as an appeal to her compassionate side.

"I didn't want to hurt him," he said. "And I really didn't want to put him back in the creek because he might not be safe from alligators and otters and other animals that might eat him."

"So, you put him in the well, huh!" she exclaimed before he could say anything else. Realizing she had him cornered, he had no choice but to fess up. "Yes ma'am," he admitted.

She told him to go drop the bucket down the well and get the fish out. He told her the fish would not cooperate by jumping into the bucket. She replied that she knew that, but he had better figure out how to do it.

He told her the only other way would be to catch it with a hook and line, but he would rather not because the hook could harm the fish. "I don't care," she told him, "You just better get that fish out of the well."

Doing as she told him, he baited a fishing pole hook with an earthworm and dropped the line down the well. The instant he felt the fish nibble, he snatched it up so that it just hooked his lip before he could swallow it, which would have killed him.

The fish he pulled from the well looked considerably larger than when it went in. It had grown bigger and fatter from eating all the bugs and insects that fell into the open well.

Although they had no scale with which to weigh it, Jimmy thought it probably weighed at least a pound, unusually large for that species of bream.

After he took it to the creek and released it, his mother told him never to put anything else in the well. "We have to drink water from it and you had a fish in it," she grumbled.

Jimmy went on his best ever fishing trip when Arthur took him deep sea fishing in the Gulf of Mexico off Panama City, Florida. Arthur had gone on several deep-sea fishing trips alone, not taking Jimmy, he told him, to avoid waking him at the early hour necessary to leave on the trip.

Jimmy believed Arthur's real reason however, to be that he thought he would get sea-sick, making him too miserable to enjoy the trip.

In spite of that, Jimmy made up his mind that when Arthur went again, it would not be without him. The next time Arthur said he planned on going deep-sea fishing the following day, Jimmy laid awake most of the night before, listening for his dad to rise and get ready to leave in the morning.

As soon as he heard sounds of stirring in the house before day light, Jimmy got up and dressed. When he went in and told Arthur he wanted to go with him, Arthur realized he had been outwitted and had no choice but to take his son along.

They drove to Panama City where Arthur bought them tickets, paying only half-price for Jimmy's, due to his young age, and boarded the deep-sea fishing boat that would take them out into the Gulf where the captain told them they would find the best fishing.

When they arrived at the destination, the rocking of the boat in the choppy water that far out kept most of the passengers too sea sick to fish, but not Jimmy and Arthur.

Arthur had fished in the Gulf often enough that it no longer bothered him. And, contrary to what Arthur probably thought, neither did it bother Jimmy, in spite of that being his first trip out.

He had no problem at all with sea sickness the entire trip. Reflecting back on it, he speculated that he might have inherited some genetic characteristic immunizing him against it.

At the captain's OK to start fishing, they dropped hand lines over the side and waited expectantly for their first bite. It wasn't long in coming.

Jimmy soon began pulling in fish weighing from a couple of pounds to 10 or 12. The half-filled container of crushed iced in which he put his catch began filling up.

He went along easily pulling them in until something he hooked wouldn't budge. Even after bracing his foot against the gunnel and tugging with all his might he could gain nothing on it.

The captain, seeing him struggle with the line, asked if he had hung up on something. He took the line and giving it a tug, it gave a little, but then shot down again as whatever held the other end fought back.

At that, the captain told him "You are not hung up, you caught a fish." After the captain pulled on it with little success, Arthur took it to see if he could make a difference.

He did at first, but after gaining a foot of line, it played back out again.

Commenting that whatever they hooked must be really big if it could overpower a grown man, Arthur strained against the line. Jimmy and the captain assisted by standing on the line Arthur managed to haul in to keep it from playing back out long enough for him to gain a few more feet.

After struggling for about an hour, they finally brought the fish to the surface. When it came into sight, the captain remarked that it looked "really big." Thinking to himself, Jimmy wondered what did he mean by "really big?"

The captain and a deckhand assisted with 2 large dip nets and a gaff hook to pull it into the boat. Once they had it on the deck the captain measured it and estimated that it weighed 75 pounds.

Jimmy marveled at the idea that a person weighing 45 or 50 pounds as he did at the time could catch a fish much heavier than himself. He seemed to recollect they called the fish a black grouper.

They took the fish home and skinned and filleted it. That being before they had refrigeration, they salted it down as their only means of preserving it. To remove the excess salt, they soaked it in a dish pan of fresh water overnight before cooking it.

Jimmy took many memorable fishing trips with his dad but never developed an interest in the sport to the extent Arthur did. As a life-long fisherman, he became a close friend and fishing companion of Red Holland, who hosted a daily fishing program broadcast by a TV station out of Dothan.

The challenge of catching the fish meant more to Arthur than eating them. He took most of what he brought home around the neighborhood and gave them away.

He became renowned throughout the wiregrass area of Alabama, Georgia and the Florida panhandle as an expert fisherman. Catching mullet on a cane pole apparently was something few people did well. But Arthur elevated it to an art unequaled by anyone else and routinely brought home coolers full of the fish that any cast or gill netter would envy.

Colin Moor, outdoor editor of the Pensacola News-Journal, wrote an article in the June 20, 1982 edition of the paper extoling Arthur's mullet fishing exploits.

Titled "Sheppard: Master Mullet hooker," it detailed Arthur's technique for getting a hook in the mouth of a fish that shuns the baits and lures that most other game fish snap up, which is why most people resort to catching mullet with nets.

Jimmy shared Arthur's love of fishing as a youngster, but what he loved more were the many pets he had on the farm.

One of them, a German shepherd named Bruno, became so beloved that the family thought of him as one of its members. When told to go get the milk cow he understood perfectly.

He ran across the pasture, fetched her to her stall in the barn and lay in the gate to keep her from getting back out until someone came to milk her. They bought a second milk cow about the time Jimmy reached 6 or 7 years old; a beautiful Jersey, she came armed with a sharp set of horns.

When she arrived on the farm, they left her to graze in the field where they had pulled the corn. Wanting Bruno to get used to rounding her up, Arthur told Jimmy to take him over to the field and teach him to put her in the pen.

She saw them coming across the field in her direction, but just stood there chewing her cud. When they got closer to her however, about 20 feet or so, she put her head down and charged them. They didn't know it but she hated kids.

Children had probably harassed or abused her at some point and she had learned to hate them as a result. She homed in on Jimmy as if intent on burying those sharp horns in his carcass so he turned and started running across the field.

When he looked over his shoulder and saw her closing on him, he knew he needed a rescue so he yelled for Bruno to get her. The dog ran up, sunk his teeth into her nose and pulled it into the dirt. She summersaulted head over heels, landing flat of her back with him lying there holding her down.

Jimmy climbed over the fence where she couldn't get at him and told Bruno to let her go. He let her up and jumped over the fence where Jimmy stood.

Thinking back on the incident, Jimmy had no doubt the dog saved his life. Bruno never liked the cow after that. If she balked when he went to round her up, he intimidated her with a menacing stare and she went anywhere he wanted her to.

Bruno, a classic black and tan of his breed, came to the Sheppards as a puppy. When full-grown he became Jimmy's close companion and protector as he demonstrated with the uppity cow.

On another occasion, Arthur took a switch to Jimmy, intending to whip him. But Bruno forced him inside to do it because on trying it outside in his presence the dog growled at him through bared teeth, as if to say you hurt him; I'll hurt you. He remained with the family when Jimmy left home for college and died of natural causes at about age 15.

Although Jimmy remembered Bruno fondly, he thought of a baby red fox that came into his possession at about age 8 as his most favorite pet.

A neighbor brought it to him after plowing it up out of a den in his field. Knowing the Sheppards were benevolent toward animals, he brought the little cub over and gave it to Jimmy. Being such a cute little fellow, Jimmy couldn't resist taking him to raise.

He fed him on a bottle and then bits of meat when he got old enough to eat. Jimmy had him for over a year during which he became full-grown with a sleek red coat. Just as a dog would, he followed Jimmy wherever he went.

In the same way dogs and cats raised together become friendly so did Bruno and the fox. At lunch time in the summer after he ate Jimmy lay on the cool linoleum floor and slept until about 2 o'clock, waiting for the mid-day heat to cool a little.

As he slept, the fox not wanting to let him out of his sight climbed onto his chest, curled up and took a nap of his own. His fondness for Jimmy at such times made him a close companion and the nicest pet a boy could ever have.

One day a family friend drove up with his hound in the truck. When the dog jumped out and saw the fox, he went after it. In fright the little animal darted toward Jimmy for protection but too late to save itself.

It had no chance when the faster long-legged hound caught it and bit the life out of it. Jimmy recalled that as one of his worst days ever.

Other pets he had included a gopher tortoise, squirrels, rabbits, alligators and baby opossums. The pleasure they gave him somewhat compensated for the pain he felt on the loss of the fox. His love of animals would remain a lifelong interest, far beyond his first 8 years.

In his 8th year his sister, Lola Frances who shared her mother's first name arrived on 24 April 1942. An accident Frances had at about age 3 caused Jimmy to get another of his few whippings from Arthur. It happened while they played in the field where peanuts had recently been harvested.

When the peanut picker ran it stripped the nuts from the plant matter consisting of leaves, stems and assorted trash and blew it out onto the ground where it accumulated in a large pile.

In disposing of it after the harvest, Arthur set it afire, which he had done that particular day. At times, the fire flamed up but sometimes only smoldered beneath the surface giving no evidence of its presence.

It looked that way to the children as they played around it but when Frances jumped into it, she fell through into a burned-out cavity beneath the surface that still smoldered. Hearing her scream in pain, Jimmy pulled her out but not before she suffered fairly serious burns on the front of her legs.

Thinking that Jimmy should have known better than to play around the burning pile, Arthur gave him a whipping. Frances recovered from the burns without major scarring and the two of them would have the full attention and affection of their parents all to themselves for several more years before having to share them with another sibling.

The seemingly idyllic life of their childhood differed dramatically from that of farm children in those places abroad where World War II raged.

That horrific affair remained so remote from their little patch of ground in south Alabama that they mostly knew nothing about it.

The war lasted from 1941 to 1945. During that time Jimmy ranged in age from 6 to 10 years old. Many of the events previously described were memories from that period but there were others as well. He listened to Roosevelt's fire side chats on the radio before they had electricity. He had never seen a radio before and it mystified him.

Trying to figure out where the voice came from, he peered around behind it and Arthur asked him what he was looking for. He replied he wanted to see how they got that man in the radio. Somebody gave them the old battery-operated radio and Arthur parked the truck by a window through which he ran battery cables to play it.

The Army never drafted Arthur because as a farmer he raised crops the country needed worse than soldiers, for which the draft board gave him a deferral. As evidence of that the selective service office stamped the letter D on his draft cards at the time he registered.

Another memory that stood out in Jimmy's mind involved a German prisoner of war who helped Arthur pick peanuts one year.

The U. S. Army brought captured German soldiers to this country to remove them far from the theater of war as a means of discouraging them from trying to escape.

Some 16 thousand of them came to Alabama and were housed in 4 major camps at Aliceville, Fort McClellan, Opelika and Fort Rucker from 1943 to 1945. Each major camp supported a number of satellite branch camps in surrounding smaller towns.

The Fort Rucker camp opened in February 1944 with a population of 2 thousand prisoners.

The same year a satellite branch camp, presumably attached to Fort Rucker due to it being the nearest major camp, opened at Dothan in a former Civilian Conservation Corps facility dating from the 1930s off State Highway 211 about 2 miles north of downtown.

As of June 2019, a retail business complex whose address was 1369 Headland Avenue occupied the site.

Germany surrendered in May 1945 and the prisoners were repatriated shortly thereafter so the POWs were only there a little over a year. Area farmers in need of workers were allowed the use of limited numbers of the prisoners as laborers on their farms.

Arthur went to the camp and picked up two of them to help with his peanut harvest in the fall of 1944 before Jimmy turned 10 years old. At the time Arthur owned a 1930s model stationary Lilliston peanut picker identical to one Jimmy has in his tractor collection.

Arthur stationed one of the prisoners at the front of the picker to load peanut vines into the hopper which fed them into the machine. The manner in which the worker held the pitchfork used in filling the hopper mattered in avoiding damage to the picker.

That required turning down the fork's curved tines in the same direction the rotating mechanical fingers pulling the plants into the picker spun. Turning the tines up in the direction opposite that of the rotating fingers would cause them to catch and damage the machine.

The German spoke no English, requiring Arthur to instruct him by demonstration and sign language in the proper use of the fork. In trying to make him understand what would happen if he turned the tines up, Arthur drew his finger across his throat in a slashing gesture signifying a shut down.

He didn't realize however, that the prisoner misinterpreted the gesture to mean he would get his throat cut if he damaged the machine and he turned pale with fright.

Having grasped Arthur's instructions, the prisoner did the job flawlessly for a couple of days. But in a distracted moment he turned the pitchfork the wrong way and as he had been warned, the picker was damaged, requiring a shut down.

Arthur had fixed it many times before. That time being no exception he had it back up and running in a couple of hours and all seemed well. The prisoner though, expecting the punishment he thought Arthur had implied looked at him fearfully and gave himself the throat slashing gesture.

When he realized the man had misunderstood, Arthur reassured him he would not get his throat cut. Dropping to his knees in great relief, he clasped his hands prayerfully, and in a language Arthur did not understand, but a demeanor he did, thanked him profusely.

Jimmy also remembered the rationing imposed on the public during the war. The government issued rationing stamps for gasoline, sugar and other items, including tires. But because they raised much of their own food and Arthur ran the ice route, they really suffered very little from rationing.

The number and kind of stamps they received depended on their occupation. Those they received in addition to food were for items necessary to the support of their activities in making a living, the gasoline Arthur needed for delivering his ice, for example.

They couldn't get sugar, which they missed the most. It became the first commodity subject to rationing when it began. Industries, businesses and commercial operations producing products requiring the use of sugar received 70 to 80 percent of their normal usage under rationing whereas individual citizens received only 50 percent.

In times of shortage, which occurred often, citizens could get none at all but bakeries, restaurants and other such establishments could if deemed essential to their business.

The public widely believed that the government favored businesses in sugar rationing to force families to buy cakes and pastries instead of making them at home. That may have been the point Arthur tried making to Jimmy about the cake under glass being made to sell.

Even though rationing often made sugar unavailable to buy, they did have an alternative to it. Jimmy's grandfather Cliff Sheppard lived on a farm between Chipley and Vernon, about 50 or 60 miles south of Rehobeth in the Florida panhandle.

In the fall of the year, Arthur and Jimmy went down and helped Cliff make cane syrup, for which they received one can out of every 3 they filled as their pay. The syrup itself and rock sugar, scraped from the bottom of recently emptied syrup cans, became their primary sweeteners when no sugar could be had.

Rock sugar, only one step away from the refined product itself, tasted nearly as good as the real thing. The artificial sweetener saccharin came out during the war and proved fairly acceptable as a sugar substitute.

When combined with a little light rock sugar it tasted pretty good; not ideal but better than straight saccharin which had an after taste to it. Unlike sugar during rationing every household had at least one gun and the Sheppards were no exception.

Like most country boys, Jimmy grew up with a gun. In addition to how to shoot it, he learned it to be a dangerous weapon that could kill or seriously injure a person if carelessly used.

Understanding that, he took safe practices seriously when handling a gun himself and when around other people using them. He enjoyed target practice and hunting with his younger brother, Buddy and a neighbor boy. When they went out hunting together their game of choice most often consisted of squirrels, quail or snipe. Jimmy thought he began unsupervised hunting with guns around 10 or 11 years old.

About the time he reached that age the REA finally arrived in Rehobeth in 1946 and strung power lines to their farm after which they wired the house to make use of the electricity.

Lacking the cash to hire an electrician for the job they did it themselves. The results might not have been up to code, had there been any, but the single 100-watt bulb dangling from the ceiling on an electric cord lit the house much brighter than the old kerosene lamps did.

The next year Jimmy graduated from the 6th grade as valedictorian, his learning ability evidently not yet diminished by poverty, contrary to liberal beliefs.

Neither had it reduced his reasoning ability for making choices in real life situations. He demonstrated that at age 12 when he browbeat his daddy into swapping his 2 mules for a tractor.

By browbeat he meant that he had enough of his mother's personality, less her temper and choice of words, to subtlety press the gentler natured Arthur into doing something if he thought it was the right thing to do.

About a year earlier, their neighbor, John Strickland, bought a Farmall Cub tractor and taught Jimmy to drive it. John told Arthur that Jimmy operated the tractor better than he could himself and had done most of his plowing.

In the short time Jimmy operated the tractor it became obvious to him even at his young age that it outperformed the mules many times over in the amount of work it did.

Although Jimmy kept "browbeating" him about how easy farming with a tractor would be Arthur never let on what he thought of the idea. That was until Jimmy came home from school one day to find a little John Deere model LA tractor sitting in the barn yard.

Unannounced, Arthur had taken the mules down to Holman Stables at Hartford and traded them in on the tractor with the implements they needed to do all of their farming. Jimmy attributed the arrival of that tractor on the farm as pivotal in bringing them out of poverty.

Occupational changes Arthur made further helped in that regard. He sold his ice route and took a job with the Kaiser Chemical Company fertilizer plant in Dothan.

At first, he only worked part-time because he could not convince himself to give up farming full-time. But

Jimmy persuaded him that with the tractor he could do the bulk of the farm work alone.

By then, Arthur had learned not to doubt anything his son said he could do. Relying on that, he decided to take a leap of faith and go full-time with Kaiser Chemical and part-time on the farm. The fertilizer plant offered job security, better pay and a better life for his family so he took that path.

Jimmy too, embarked on a new path of sorts when on the night he graduated as 6th grade valedictorian he went to school for the first time not dressed in overalls, but wore a suit instead.

He may never have dressed as nicely as Little Lord Fauntleroy, as he put it, but always kept neat and clean in the clothes he wore. They were country clothes including his home-made shirts which his mother sewed from flour sacks.

They bought flour in 25-pound bags made of print cotton cloth. When empty, his mother ripped the seams open so they spread out in square sheets.

She washed them and using a shirt pattern, probably from Sears and Roebuck, cut the cloth with scissors and sewed the shirt together on her sewing machine.

With making clothes for their families being nothing unusual among country homemakers then, many of them became so skilled at it that they produced clothes as good, or better, than store-bought ones; Lola being no exception.

After making Jimmy's shirts she starched and ironed each one before he put them on. Likewise, she starched and ironed his overalls with a crease down the legs. She took pride in his appearance, combing his hair and seeing to his cleanliness, especially his ears, in the mornings before he left for school.

She gaged how well he washed by inspecting his ears, and if he wanted to pass her scrutiny, he knew to scrub them with a bath cloth the first thing every morning until spotless.

With electricity, he had better light to see if his ears met muster and it made his studying at night easier. It did not however, solve all the problems of the house that would qualify it as the home of an impoverished family today.

Its draftiness from cracks between the vertical wall boards through which Jimmy could lie in bed and see day-light rendered it a cold place to sleep and study in winter. The only heat in the house came from the fireplace and kitchen stove.

Today it would qualify for a tax payer funded weatherization grant which would pay all the costs of replacing drafty windows and covering the walls to seal the cracks. Not to mention the installation of gas or electric heat in every room.

Back then the Sheppards' felt fortunate in having a compassionate and generous landlord in the person of Jim Jones thoughtful enough to provide them with covering that blocked the cracks in the walls.

Made of material similar to asphalt roofing shingles, it came in rolls of sheeting about 3 or 4 feet wide which they installed themselves. Its design on the outside simulated a brick wall in appearance.

It might be argued that being their landlord obligated Jones to do what he reasonably could to make the house more livable for his tenants. But they saw it as an act of generosity that made him more than just a landlord to them.

He became a close family friend and visited often from Dothan. He took a special interest in Jimmy's education and made it a ritual to see his latest report card every time he stopped by.

Jimmy took as much pleasure in showing it to him as he did in seeing it. By making consistently high grades, that became paramount in what his parents expected of him.

Early on he got the impression that if his parents and Jim Jones considered his grades important, they must be serious business. If they thought it was the right thing to do, how could he not pay attention to them. That always motivated him to keep trying his best.

Attempting his best at least, became his goal in everything he did, even learning to drive a truck. When he reached 13, John Strickland, who allowed him to cut his tractor driving teeth on his Farmall Cub, bought a brand-new red Diamond T truck, a big 2-ton model.

As he had done with his tractor, he put Jimmy behind the wheel as soon as he grasped its operating basics, which he did in a matter of minutes. When they worked in the fields during planting season Jimmy hauled in seeds and fertilizer on the truck.

At harvest time, he brought in the truck and loaded it with peanuts from the picker. He filled the bed with loose peanuts level with the top of the high side panels. He then ringed the perimeter of the side panels with burlap bags full of peanuts laid on their sides end-to end to form another level of containment.

After topping off that space with loose peanuts, he had 5 tons on a truck rated for only 2. When he drove it across the field it creaked and groaned from the swaying of the bed under the massive load it carried.

To minimize the instability, he could drive no faster than a crawl until he reached the smoother and firmer ground of the road.

He had gained enough experience from driving the loaded truck on the farm that when he put it on the road, he had absolute confidence in his ability to handle it, not apprehensive in the least.

Sitting on 2 pillows to see past the steering wheel, he regularly hauled loads to the peanut mill in Dothan. He drove the 20-mile round trip over dirt roads as competently as any grown man could have.

He liked the idea of driving on the paved roads better, but the risk of state troopers stopping and citing him as an unlicensed driver restrained him from doing so. Driving on the dirt roads put him at less risk of that because state troopers rarely ever patrolled them.

He drove Arthur's pickup without a license over those same roads when using it to market vegetables. During the war Eleanor Roosevelt proclaimed planting victory gardens as everybody's patriotic duty.

No less patriotic than anyone else, the Sheppards did not think of gardening in that light. They did it to survive.

Near the end of the war and afterwards it became a third addition to their cash crops.

Jimmy hauled the excess they didn't eat or preserve in Mason jars to Dothan and peddled them off the back of the pickup.

They used money from that source to buy many things they needed but acquired other necessities without money. They had 2 milk cows and when both freshened at the same time, they had more milk, butter and butter milk than they could use. The same went for eggs from the chickens.

That gave Lola enough excess dairy products and eggs to sell on the rolling store when it came by on Tuesdays. In exchange for those items, she received an equal dollar amount of the few things they couldn't raise on the farm like flour, sugar, salt, her dipping snuff and Arthur's Prince Albert smoking tobacco.

They also made a few dollars off the milk cows' calves they sold after weaning and raising as yearlings. They didn't butcher their own beef, but they did their hogs.

Done in the winter time to keep the meat fresh, and no blow flies were around to spoil it, Jimmy rolled it in a salt trough to give it a preservative coating. He next hung it in the smoke house, suspended from overhead poles, to which he tied the meat with strips of tough bear grass.

As part of that job, he kept the green oak or hickory wood smoldering on the dirt floor so it gave off more smoke than flames. After curing, they put the meat in a cold storage bin at the ice plant in Dothan they rented for a small fee of 3 or 4 dollars a year.

A single bin held the meat of up to 4 hogs. They were lucky in supplying their own pork. It could not be bought when the country's entire commercial production of both pork and beef were required in filling the military's war time needs.

That requirement had ended by the time Jimmy started driving but many people seemed to prefer home cured pork to that sold commercially.

He learned that on one of his vegetable selling trips. As he left for town with a fresh load, his mother told him to pick up a couple of hams from the cold storage plant.

After retrieving them from the bin he laid them in the pickup bed with the vegetables. A woman stopping by to look at his vegetables saw the hams and told him she wanted to buy one. He declined however, telling her his family needed them for their own use.

She told him if he would sell her half a ham, she would buy everything else he had on the pickup. Curious as to why she would do that, he asked and she told him because she wanted the ham. Not batting an eye when he told her he wanted 12 dollars for the vegetables, she took the whole lot and went happily on her way.

When he got home and told his mother about it, she told him he shouldn't have because it may leave them without enough to last until winter when they could butcher more hogs.

The next time he went to the cold storage plant he counted the hams, sides and shoulders left in the bin. He told Lola how many there were and deciding it enough to last out the season she told him to go ahead and sell a couple more hams.

The woman who bought all his vegetables conditioned on his selling her the ham had given him an idea. He took the meat to the grocery store and had it cut into quarter inch thick slices.

He then offered his vegetable customers two deals; 1 slice of ham for every 5 pounds of vegetables they bought, or 2 slices for every 10 pounds they bought. It went over so well that he sold the entire pickup load of vegetables at his first stop in no time at all. It tickled the customers to get the ham and it tickled him to empty the pickup so fast.

All the work he could do with the tractor tickled him even more. Thanks to it, the farming had never been better. With its greater productivity and without the less productive mules to feed he had cut back considerably on the corn acreage while increasing that planted to the cash crops of cotton and peanuts.

He grew the corn as feed for the milk cows, chickens and hogs, and to have ground into meal for the family's cornbread. If not for that, he would have planted no corn at all.

He and the neighbor, John Strickland, helped each other out to their mutual benefit. John loaned his Diamond T truck to Jimmy for hauling his peanuts and cotton to market and Jimmy used his John Deere to help John do his plowing.

Any time he drove the tractor he focused solely on the job at hand. He learned the importance of that when his failure to pay proper attention caused him to damage the tractor he drove.

It belonged to an uncle who asked him to do some of his plowing. The tractor, a John Deere, tricycle-wheeled model MT, and his were identical. An electric utility pole stood in the middle of the field he worked.

The pole had a guy wire attached to it and being so intent on not hitting the wire he failed to notice the end of the rear axle stuck out beyond the wheel too far to clear the pole. He ran the tractor in third gear and when the tip of the axel struck the pole it cracked the cast iron housing of the transmission.

Damaging his uncle's tractor upset him more than anything he had ever done in his life and he could not quit apologizing for it.

Fortunately, they found a welder expert enough at brazing cast iron to successfully repair the tractor. He did such a good job that the uncle continued using the tractor for the rest of his life without any problems from the repaired crack.

Jimmy never forgot that and it made him even more careful with his own tractor. He understood the importance of the tractor to his family's livelihood and made every effort possible to avoid doing anything to it that would put their wellbeing at risk.

Beyond his responsible use of the tractor, Jimmy believed his family would benefit from relieving them of as much of the most stressful work on the farm as possible.

Picking cotton topped the list and Jimmy wised up to the idea that he could hire out that back-breaking job to black field hands. The day before bringing them in, he parked a wagon in the cotton patch with the weighing scales mounted on it.

The next morning, he got up before daylight and drove to Dothan to pick up a crew of pickers looking to earn some money. He brought them to the farm and put them to work in the cotton field. During the day he plied them generously with ice water.

At lunch time he fed them a sumptuous meal prepared just for them by his mother, unequaled by anyone in the community for her gastronomic exploits. In other words, a damned good cook. Energized with full bellies and refreshing ice water, they made short work of Jimmy's 10-acre cotton patch.

At quitting time every evening, Jimmy loaded them on the truck and hauled them back to Dothan with money in their pockets. On returning to the farm, he hitched the wagon load of cotton to the tractor and hauled it to the Malvern gin recently built just a short 3 miles away.

In only a few days, he had his cotton harvested. Not only had he spared his family from that despised chore, but it freed him up to work at the Dothan gin to earn a little extra money.

At the height of the harvesting season the gin needed all the help it could hire to keep the glut of cotton coming in all at once from building into a major backlog. Jimmy worked there seasonally from about age 12 to 14.

In spite of his slight build, he did well the job given him of transferring on a hand truck 5-hundred-pound bales of cotton from the press to the warehouse.

The secret he learned, depended not on physical strength, but good technique. The man who taught him the job demonstrated how to do it.

He showed him that by getting the bale rocking from side to side and keeping it going in a steady rhythm he could "walk" it anywhere on the warehouse floor he wanted it to go. He "hung" and weighed the bales and cut samples from each, which he wrapped in brown paper for grading purposes.

He then hand trucked each bale to the back of the warehouse where he dumped it in time to return and catch the next one rolling out of the press about every 8 minutes. He worked at it 72 hours a week, which broke down to 12 hours a day, 6 days a week.

Their growing income from the farm, part-time work and Arthur's full-time job at the fertilizer plant enabled them to buy the farm the year Jimmy turned 15.

They financed it with a 43-hundred-dollar handshake loan Arthur received from Mr. Lester Godwin who lived near Rehobeth. Repaying it in installments, Arthur had the debt zeroed out by the time Jimmy graduated from high school.

Except for the 6 years Jim Jones owned it, that put ownership of the farm back in the Sheppard family going back over a hundred years.

The same year they took out the mortgage, Jimmy graduated from the 9th grade. On becoming a sophomore, he exchanged his overalls for more stylish Levi jeans as his preferred school attire.

He dressed the same way for church, which he stopped attending because he disagreed with something said to him in Sunday school at the Baptist church where his parents went.

The Sunday school teacher told him God loved us, would be good to us, and keep us. The next Sunday, he said you need to fear the Lord because if you don't do his bidding you will go to hell and burn forever.

Jimmy raised his hand and said, "Preach, you told us last Sunday that God loved us unconditionally but this Sunday you tell us if we don't do his will, we will burn in hell forever. It can be one way or the other but it can't be both ways."

The Sunday school teacher told him he needed to go home and get his thinking straight and not come back until he did. Taking his advice, Jimmy never went back.

That marked the beginning of his transition to spiritual progression rather than listening to the preachers and the point at which he started breaking away from the church. He tried other churches after that but found none of them to his liking.

In med school he had a Catholic roommate with whom he attended church because he didn't own his own car at the time and knew of no other church he could attend within walking distance.

Unhappy with that experience, he thought if the Baptists, Methodists and Presbyterians had it wrong, the Catholics were even worse. Because of his disenchantment with organized religion, he stopped attending church altogether for a time.

But while still in school, he viewed attendance just the opposite. Arthur and Lola insisted he never miss school unless illness kept him out. He took that advice just as seriously as he took his grades and other than 8 days in the 1st grade when he came down with the measles, he never missed another day from the 2nd grade to the 12th.

Although against his nature to do so, he justifiably could have claimed bragging rights for his perfect attendance from grade 6 to graduation from junior high at grade 9. But closing out his freshman year as a repeating valedictorian may have been a feat unmatched by any student up to that time in the school's history.

Modern liberal childhood education theorists would have found that astounding. Poor children excelling in education without massive government intervention to them is an oxymoron. At that point, nay saying liberals would have bet against Jimmy's chances of repeating his excellent performance a third time.

He began thinking of going to college while in high school. Their old land lord, Jim Jones with his unwavering interest in Jimmy's grades kept the idea alive in his head.

Jones had a son who went to medical school and became a physician. Jimmy had never thought of doctors as regular people educated in medicine. He thought they were kind of like kings; born, not made. But that planted the idea in his mind that he might like to go to college and become a doctor himself.

Jim encouraged him every time he came out to see his report card. He praised him as smart, for making good grades, for being number 1 in his class and capable of doing whatever he wanted in life.

Jimmy asked him if he thought he should go to college and Jones told him yes, he should. Jim proved a benevolent and kind gentleman because he helped them in every way he could and never missed an opportunity to encourage Jimmy in his education.

When Jimmy made valedictorian, Jim gave him gifts as tokens of admiration for making good grades and to keep him motivated.

Anything that lifts morale and points to a brighter future tends to motivate and the prospect of a new home put the Sheppards in that state of mind when they bought the farm in 1949.

Unlike when they could not afford a piece of cake under glass, their rising income put a new home within their reach. They had a sizable number of tall pine trees growing in the cow pasture which Jimmy thought would yield most of the lumber needed in building a house.

He and Arthur felled the trees with a cross cut saw and hauled the logs to the mill for sawing into lumber. They used that plus some they bought to give them the amount they needed in building a 1 thousand square foot home which Jimmy designed. Located a short distance from the old house, they built the wood frame structure on concrete block piers and topped it with tin.

They walled it initially in rough lumber, but later covered the wood with white asbestos shingles. Not only did it have electricity; but they had a well drilled and an electric water pump installed, so that for the first time they had indoor plumbing.

But like the cake, air conditioning as well as an indoor toilet remained unaffordable luxuries and the outhouse along with summer-time discomfort familiar from their old home followed them to the new one.

Although those aspects of life in the new house were little different than in the old one, just changing from the dreariness of the old place to the fresh look, feel and smell of the new home could not help but raise family spirits.

Neither did it hurt anyone's feelings as the heat of summer waned with the promise of fall soon to follow and a new school term as well.

Jimmy had competent teachers at Rehobeth. Most of them did their jobs well although limited in the courses they could offer simply because the small school's meager budget forced it to stress basic education courses.

It could not afford to hire the additional instructors needed to teach more advanced courses such as algebra and geometry.

The same applied to the sciences. Instead of individual courses such as botany and biology, they only offered a general science course that combined those and others which did little more than introduce and summarize what each of the disciplines involved.

The courses they offered in bookkeeping, typing and the vocational classes in agriculture, horticulture, and animal husbandry focused on preparing graduates for employment directly out of high school rather than for higher education.

In his 3 years of high school vocational agriculture classes the only skills he learned even remotely related to his future career were how to castrate male pigs and calves and treat screw worm infestations.

But the knowledge of suturing he picked up in connection with those skills did prove beneficial to him later on. One day in med school while assisting a surgeon by handing him operating instruments, the surgeon finally just handed Jimmy the needle and thread and told him to finish up.

Later the surgeon asked him where he learned how to do that. Jimmy told him about the surgery he did on pigs and bull calves when castrating them on the farm. Back then the maggot-like screw worm put livestock with open wounds at risk because it fed on live flesh. If not treated the infestation gradually worsened leading to the animal's death.

The worms hatched from the eggs of a fly that laid them in open wounds of warm-blooded animals. The insect made no distinction between humans and other animals when seeking a host for its parasitic offspring. That put humans at risk also, especially infants in whose noses the flies laid their eggs leading to nasal and sinus cavity infestations.

Treatment of animals involved cleaning the maggots out of the wound, applying stock dip as an antiseptic and suturing it up. Infested humans of course required the care of a physician.

In 1958, a decades long government program culminated in eradication of the screw worm fly in the southeastern U. S., where they caused the greatest damage. That saved livestock producers millions of dollars in losses and ended the necessary treatment and suturing of animals that Jimmy recalled.

The idea he would ever suture a human patient never entered his mind when he hauled farm crops and vegetables to Dothan as an unlicensed driver.

By the time he reached the legal driving age of 16 in December of 1950 he had many hours of solid driving under his belt and looked forward to legitimacy so he could drive on the highway. In preparation for the big day, he asked Arthur to come to the school at lunch and take him to Dothan to get his driver's license.

Agreeing to it, Arthur told him to watch out the back door of the school and be ready to go when he got there. Arthur arrived and took him, and after he passed the test and received his license, drove him back to school.

As he walked in the building on returning, Principal William McNeal met him at the back door and asked if he got his license. When he replied yes, the principal told him to go get bus number 36; he needed a driver for it.

So began his high school bus driving career that lasted until the day he graduated. He never put a scratch on it, never had a flat tire, and never injured a child. That first year he did all his driving on dirt roads, which he suspected the principal almost certainly had planned.

No glass could be slicker than some of those roads when it rained. As he drove down a wet clay hill once, the bus suddenly skidded, spun around 180 degrees and ended up pointing in the direction from which he had come.

The narrow road made turning it back around on the spot too risky, requiring him to drive back up the hill, pull into somebody's yard with room to reverse directions and continue on.

Jimmy guessed the principal knew he drove proficiently before putting him in charge of the bus. Few people in Rehobeth were unaware he regularly drove a heavy truck to and from Dothan since being barely old enough to see past the steering wheel.

The principal knew, and figured if he could drive that truck, he could just as easily handle a school bus. When the high school band attended camp at Panama City Beach the principal tapped Jimmy as driver of the bus taking them on the trip.

It just so happened he played lead snare drummer in the band as well. That showed a great deal of trust in the responsibility of a boy only 16 years old at the time and spoke highly of the school principal's confidence in him.

The same could not be said however, of a few of the parents whose children rode his bus. A group of them complained to the principal implying that Jimmy's young age somehow disqualified him from driving the bus on a busy section of Highway 231 along which they lived.

The principal told them he would give Jimmy a 30-day trial period during which if any complaints about his driving arose, he would consider making changes. But when the time expired no one had complained, leaving him free to continue driving the bus as he had been assigned.

Getting his driver's license ranked among the most memorable events of his 16th year. But the birth of his little brother, Arthur Robert, topped the list. He arrived on 28 October 1950, a little over a month before Jimmy's birthday the following December. At that point Arthur had not named one of his children after himself, so he bestowed the honor on his second son.

Jimmy and his little brother, "Buddy," as he nicknamed him, became inseparable. From the time Buddy could walk until Jimmy left home for college, the 2 of them seldom remained apart. Even when plowing on the tractor Jimmy would have Buddy sitting on his lap holding him tight with one arm and steering the tractor with the other.

Buddy found the arrangement so comforting that not even the loud pop, pop, popping of the 2 cylinder "popping John" tractor engine could keep him from falling asleep as the ride continued, sometimes for hours on end.

At some point after Buddy's birth, it dawned on Jimmy that Buddy had come along 8 years after Frances, and she had come along 8 years after himself. Recognizing it as something of a pattern, he wondered if the equal year intervals were intentional or coincidental. His curiosity getting the better of him, he asked his mother which it was.

She replied that they spaced them like that so the older ones could mind the little ones while the parents worked on the farm during the depression when it took the entire family working together to scrape by.

It amused him to think that the only flaw in that logic was that as the first-born child the absence of an older sibling babysitter had made him a basket case.

He continued juggling school, bus driving and farming with none of them negatively impacting the other. The farming had gotten easier due to the newer two-row model MT John Deere Arthur traded the old tractor in on the previous year. When not in school or driving the bus, Jimmy worked on the farm.

He finished his route with the bus about 4 o'clock in the afternoon. After parking it he changed clothes and climbed on the tractor. From then until Arthur came home from the fertilizer plant, he turned more ground with the John Deere in an hour than the mules could in a day. About 8:30 or 9:00 at night after his supper, Arthur relieved him and kept plowing until about 10:30.

When Arthur took over Jimmy went home and did his school work. They followed that routine until he graduated from high school and went off to college.

As a bare foot farm boy before his high school days, he looked back on another routine that reminded him of the benefits of wearing shoes. Just as sure as spring, summer and fall came, so did the inevitable hookworm infestations afflicting him during those times simply because he liked the freedom of going shoeless.

The first symptoms appeared with the ground itch caused by the microscopic nematodes burrowing through the skin of his feet on their way to invading his gut. He took the treatments required in ridding himself of them from ages 4 to 15.

He accepted that as the price he paid for the pleasure of going naked from the ankles down between April and December every year. He finally reached the age however, when he found not wearing shoes less preferable than wearing them.

Playing football and marching in the band made them mandatory. Football earned him a broken nose and deviated septum, which price he paid for filling a slot on the team that required greater athleticism than his physique enabled him to deliver.

That happened because the coach ran out of the best players he could find in the school's small student body before he had filled all 11 position. After that, he had to settle for the next best available players in making a full roster, and Jimmy made the team on that basis.

Other than being fast of foot, he lacked the size and strength needed for a good football player. But what he lacked in athletic ability he made up for in school spirit, enthusiasm and as in everything else he did, the determination to put forth his best effort in playing the game.

Regardless of Jimmy's abilities, and of any of the other players, the coach knew he needed to keep every position manned in maintaining a viable squad.

If he lost even one player, the scarcity at the school of qualified or willing replacements might make filling the vacancy difficult or impossible, putting the future of the school's football program at risk. It would also put the coach's career at risk, a position in which no coach wants to find himself.

Recognizing that, Jimmy's coach knew he had to give his players considerable leeway in what he would allow them to do.

That became evident when he gave Jimmy the choice of either playing on the team or marching in the band, both of which he did during football games.

When Jimmy told him that given the choice, he would take the band the coach relented and allowed him to continue as the only student in the school pulling that double duty.

In managing the two he played football in the first half of the game, changed into his band uniform to perform with the band at half time and re-dressed for football to finish out the game.

The coach's willingness to allow Jimmy to continue with what he did in football and band demonstrated the mutual respect that existed between the students and teachers at the school.

That relationship however, sometimes became frayed, as once happened to Jimmy in study hall. He sat at a table trying to finish his homework to give himself more time for plowing that evening after school.

His friend, Foster Watkins, sitting across the table from him, asked to borrow his pencil. Without looking up, he patted around on the front of his shirt until he found the pencil in his pocket and handed it across the table. At the same time, he said a little too loudly, "here it is." Ms. Dawsey, a red-headed teacher in charge of study hall that period, overheard him.

Calling his name in a scolding voice, she asked if she had given him permission to speak. Before thinking, he shot back "No ma'am, but I didn't ask you either, did I?" Other students in the study hall, who had been quite as a mouse up to that point, burst into raucous laughter.

That so angered the teacher that she ordered him straight to the principal's office. Knowing he had stepped in over his head he told her, "Yes ma'am." He got up and walked down the hall to face the same principal who put him behind the wheel of a school bus.

On entering, the principal asked what he needed. Reaching back and pushing the door shut behind himself, he told him he had something bad to confess. The principal asked what it was and he told him the story.

Spinning his chair around with his back to Jimmy and clamping his hand over his mouth, the principal's entire 6-foot 2-inch, 250-pound frame convulsed in shoulder shaking hilarity.

Momentarily he regained his composure and turned back around. In feigned solemnity, he told Jimmy "That was not a very nice thing to say, was it?" Jimmy said "No sir," and the principal told him "OK, go on back to study hall."

Jimmy knew he had better tell his parents about it before it got back to them from somebody else, which he did when he got home that afternoon. On hearing it, Arthur remained silent.

Lola on the other hand, ever the disciplinarian, told him she thought he would know better than to say such a ridiculous thing to a school teacher.

While enrolled in high school vocational agriculture classes, Jimmy participated in the FFA (Future Farmers of America) program. Officially known as the National FFA Organization, it is "An American 501(c) (3) youth organization, specifically a career and technical student organization, based on middle and high school classes that promote and support agricultural education.

It probably would not be an exaggeration to say that every rural high school in the United States at one time participated in the FFA.

Well-known people who were its members include Jimmy Carter, Rick Perry, Johnny Cash, Steve Doocey (Fox News), Trace Adkins, Toby Keith, Willie Nelson, and Taylor Swift, to name only a very few.

A large number of people prominent in politics, entertainment, the arts and other occupations have gone through its ranks.

A part of being in the FFA in high school required its members to carry out a project approved by the agriculture teacher. Jimmy chose growing an acre of corn and determining its yield as his project.

Laying out an acre accordingly, he fertilized it with manure from the mule and cow stalls. He planted the corn, cultivated it as appropriate and let it grow to maturity. When harvest time came, he told his teacher he thought it would yield at least 75 bushels to the acre.

To determine the estimated yield, he harvested one of the 24 rows in the plot and counted the number of bushels. He then multiplied that number times 24 which gave a calculated yield in excess of a hundred bushels per acre, far above the average yield of 30 to 40 bushels typical of most small southern farms at the time.

He attributed the higher production to the natural organic fertilizer he used which contained more potent nutrients than the commonly used manufactured chemical fertilizer. A good year weather-wise that brought sufficient rain played no small role in the in the project's high yield.

Just as plentiful rain is good for a crop, so too is a positive relationship with a dedicated teacher beneficial to a student. Jimmy's high school teacher, James Ballard, played that role in his life. He, like Jim Jones, encouraged Jimmy to do his best in school and go on to college.

Due to his advice, Jimmy decided on going to the University of Alabama at Tuscaloosa. He suggested it rather than Troy or Auburn, which were Jimmy's first choices.

The university, he believed, better prepared its graduates for higher levels of education than the other two, making them more acceptable to schools offering professional degrees.

Such schools especially welcomed applicants with excellent academic records. As he had done in grades 6 and 9, Jimmy earned recognition for an unprecedented 3rd time as valedictorian on graduation from Rehobeth High School the evening of Friday, 29 May, 1953.

That accomplishment by a poor south Alabama farm boy without government intervention would have present day liberals passing out in the isles from exasperated disbelief.

Principal McNeal told him that after reviewing his grades, he found them to be the highest of any student on record in the hundred years of the school's existence.

Hearing that news made Jimmy proud, but the fear of appearing immodest if he shared it with others restrained him from doing so. It is doubtful however, that those who supported and encouraged him throughout his first 12 years of school would have felt that way if he had told them.

Conspicuously absent among those encouraging Jimmy to go to college, as surprising as it may seem, were his parents.

They did not object to his going, but offered no encouragement simply because they could not afford to send him. They feared that after he got started and ran out of money, he would suffer a major disappointment on having to quit. The weekend before he left, his mother begged him in tears not to go for that reason.

Her tears failed to dissuade him because he deeply believed going to college was the right thing for him to do. The following Monday, Jim Jones picked him up in his new Oldsmobile and drove him to Tuscaloosa. He helped him enroll in classes and get settled in the dorm. Jimmy paid his tuition and other costs for the summer term with the money he had saved from his high school bus driving pay.

II

≈TUSCALOOSA≈

And on to
UAB School of Medicine, Marriage, the Air
Force, Volkswagen and Gatorade.

When admitted to the University of Alabama at Tuscaloosa the registrar informed Jimmy that his high school record limited his acceptance as conditional.

The reason being that he lacked completion of certain high school science and math courses required as prerequisites to entry level college course work.

It seems contradictory that a high school valedictorian would fall short of those standards, but it was due to no fault of his own. In reality, the blame lay with Rehobeth High School who failed to meet his needs with a curriculum deficient in the required courses.

That meant he would spend his first year of college completing the remedial high school courses he lacked before he could enroll in courses required for credit toward a degree.

After enrolling and settling in at Tuscaloosa, he would soon learn the depths of the loyalty and friendship of his former high school teacher, James Ballard. James knew of Jimmy's close-knit relationship with his family.

He feared the college-imposed separation from them might so overwhelm Jimmy with homesickness that he would quit school and return home. There might be less chance of that he thought if he could help Jimmy resist the impulse.

As a competent and dedicated teacher, James also recognized the value of continuing professional education. He saw at that moment an opportunity to enhance his professional training and support his former student at the same time by enrolling at the University for a summer refresher course.

Jimmy admitted if not for that gesture, the absence of a familiar face and friend at Tuscaloosa that first term would have indeed led him to quit and go home.

He already held James Ballard in high esteem from their relationship in high school and that act cemented him in Jimmy's mind as the most inspirational person in his life. His gratitude toward James ran so deep that at the birth of his only son, he named him Ballard.

At the time he enrolled at the university Jimmy had sufficient funds to cover tuition and all other expenses except the last 5 weeks of the meal plan.

As the end of the paid-up meal period approached, he realized he would have to drop out and work until he earned enough money to re-enroll.

Faced with that decision he went to the dean's office to withdraw so that he would get incompletes in his courses instead of Fs. The dean looked at his transcript and seeing his excellent grades, asked his reason for leaving.

Jimmy told him he had exhausted his funds and planned on working temporarily with a local housing contractor to earn the money he needed after which he would be back. Noting he only lacked 5 weeks to the end of the semester the dean asked how much he needed. Jimmy told him 150 dollars for a meal ticket.

Opening his desk drawer, the dean, a Mr. Adams, pulled out his personal check book and wrote a check for the amount. Jimmy took it and finished out the term. After the semester ended, he took the job with the building contractor.

When he received his first pay check he paid the dean back. Dean Adams told him he thought he would do that and was why he did not hesitate to write him the check.

That proved to be only the first of many charitable acts of great generosity and kindness bestowed on Jimmy during his many years of college, without which he could never have afforded.

Recognizing Jimmy's extraordinary potential as well as his lack of resources the dean expressed an interest in helping him. He told Jimmy a professor he knew had a spare bedroom which he could use for the upcoming college term.

The only thing required of him in exchange would be to babysit the professor's child when he and his wife attended social functions. With a younger sister and brother back home, Jimmy knew about babysitting and accepted the offer without hesitation. That charitable act secured his lodging for the second year of premed school but not the third.

Due to the professor's wife being an expectant mother, they needed the spare bedroom for the new addition to their family. Jimmy earned enough money to pay his tuition and expenses for the year by working at the university and substitute teaching the Chemistry I lab. class.

As his third year of college approached with no prospects of funds to pay for it, his professors again came through for him. They arranged a meeting with Norman and Helene Hibbard who expressed an interest in helping him.

Norm, an ex-marine, had served honorably in that branch of service. Helene held a law degree and served as an officer of Gulf States Paper Corporation of Tuscaloosa.

As the daughter of Herbert D. and Mildred Westervelt Warner and granddaughter of Herbert E. Westervelt, founder of the corporation, she came from a long line of wealthy philanthropists. Her brother, Jack Warner, served as president and CEO of the company, which owned 37 thousand acres of pine timber in Alabama and two paper mills.

His professors no doubt had already filled them in on Jimmy's background as a poor farm boy with enormous potential at risk of going to waste without the financial support he needed to get through college and medical school.

After meeting him and deciding to give him a chance to prove himself, the Hibbards offered not only full sponsorship of his college education costs but all his living expenses as well, including coming to live in their home with them.

When they made him the offer, Jimmy at first did not comprehend their intentions, thinking they expected repayment. He thanked them for their kindness, but said he could not accept because it would be impossible for him to ever pay them back.

On recognizing their sincerity when told accepting their assistance would place him under no obligation to repay, it humbled him as the most overwhelming generosity ever offered him in his life.

Moving into their home, he described it as looking like a grand castle on a hill overlooking the Black Warrior River. They owned a yacht which they docked on the river.

The company owned an airplane available to them for business or personal use. They also had access to a company owned vacation property at Ponte Vedra Beach on the Atlantic Ocean south of Jacksonville, Florida which Norm piloted the family to and from in the airplane. At their home on the river, they had 2 servants in the house and 1 in the yard.

When Jimmy mentioned working while in college, the Hibbards would not hear of it, insisting he continue his studies full-time and leave his tuition and other expenses to them.

With their assurance of support, he stayed in school year-round because by doing so he could graduate from pre-med school sooner than if he limited attendance to the fall and winter terms only.

He took occasional breaks in his studies though and accompanied the Hibbards to their second home at Ponte

Vedra Beach. If he needed to go home for some reason, Norm would fly him in the airplane to the airport in Dothan where family or friends would pick him up for transport to the location of his choice.

The Hibbards treated him like royalty. Norm even took him down to the local Pontiac dealership at Christmas, and walking over to a sporty red and white convertible on the showroom floor, offered to buy it for him.

He told Jimmy he needed transportation more reliable than the bicycle he rode back and forth to the university every day. Feeling in his heart that accepting a gift of that magnitude on top of what this family had done for him already would be an unappreciative abuse of their abundant generosity; Jimmy felt compelled to reject it.

He told Norm he had been too good to him already; that they had helped him more than he could help himself. He said they had done far, far more for him than they should have. Telling him of his gratitude from the bottom of his soul, he said please don't do this.

Norm replied that he wanted to give him the car for Christmas but if he didn't want him to, he wouldn't. Jimmy told him he deeply appreciated the offer but would rather he not do it and let him continue on as he had been doing, to which Norm said OK, and that ended it.

When asked why he thought people had been so gracious and generous to him, Jimmy replied modestly that he had never known anybody with old wealth that wasn't that way.

Every time he got his grade sheet, the Hibbards asked to see it. Vocally impressed with the consistently high marks on it, they would just shake their heads in amazement and tell him to keep on with what he was doing.

Just as it had for Jim Jones, James Ballard and Dean Adams, his academic excellence as evidenced on his grade reports elicited the Hibbards' charitable urges toward him.

To Jimmy's good fortune in threading his way through academia, he crossed paths at those times most crucial to financing his education with people who thought academic excellence truly deserved rewarding. The Hibbards were among the wealthy elite who not only believed that, but had the resources to act on it in a significant way.

The enormity of what they did for him far outweighed anything he could do for them. In recognition of that, he acquiesced to their wants of him at every opportunity.

They had 2 children in need of babysitting on occasion and Jimmy was most happy to provide that service as a gesture of his appreciation. He kept the children, sometime when Norm and Helene were away for a week or more.

During those times, he went in the mornings to pick up the house maids whose jobs with the Hibbards were during the day only, and delivered them back home at the end of their work day.

On those trips the children accompanied him and on their return home from the evening trip, he fed and bathed them and put them to bed. Their names were Billy, age 3 and Helene, age 4 or 5.

Once, Billy was giving his mother a hard time about something and she asked him if he ever told Jimmy no when he kept them. He said of course not. She then asked why he said no to her. He replied that Jimmy is different.

When she asked if he wanted her to go get Jimmy, he said no; he would do what she asked him to. Helene, the mother, told Jimmy that story, saying they would do things for him that they would not do for their parents. She asked him why that was.

He replied that he just treated them like kids; they had a close relationship and liked each other. That is obvious, she told him in response.

During his time with the Hibbards, Jimmy became acquainted with Dr. Douglass Haisten, a general practitioner in Dothan.

They became close friends and Jimmy dated his daughter for a time. Jimmy also introduced the doctor to the Hibbards which led to a collaboration between he and Norm in accommodating Jimmy's transportation needs.

Jimmy overheard the doctor tell Norm that he would come pick him up if he ever needed to come home when it was inconvenient for Norm to bring him.

As Jimmy neared the end of his third year at Tuscaloosa, Dr. Haisten advised him to go ahead and apply for admission to the University of Alabama School of Medicine at Birmingham.

He suggested that by applying early he would have time to take any courses med-school required that he had not yet completed.

Following Dr. Haisten's advice, Jimmy applied and to his surprise the medical school agreed to admit him a year short of earning his pre-med bachelor's degree. That rarely granted privilege came in recognition of his induction into the Phi Beta Kappa Society.

They would allow him to complete the required fourth year of his bachelor's degree during the first year of medical school. Of the 80 students UAB accepted that year, Jimmy counted himself among less than a half dozen who held that distinction.

His sooner-than-expected acceptance at UAB medical school came as good and bad news to Jimmy. When he went home and informed Dr. Haisten of his acceptance, he gave him the bad news that he had no way to pay for it.

Once again, in Dr. Haisten, Jimmy had happened upon a person who believed strongly that academic excellence deserved rewarding and the good doctor had both the conviction and resources to, "put his money where his mouth was."

The gloom accompanying the bad news turned to sunshine when Dr. Haisten pulled out his check book and handed it to Jimmy telling him in so many words he could do with it as he pleased.

Jimmy offered strongly felt objections as to why he should not accept it but in the end relented on the doctor's insistence that he should.

For all intents and purposes that solved Jimmy's money problems through the end of medical school. In addition to having access to his check book, every time he visited, the doctor would pull out his wallet and put 2 or 3 hundred dollars of cash in Jimmy's hand.

Feeling he should account for all he received from Dr. Haisten, Jimmy maintained a record book in which he meticulously wrote everything down. Of all those who contributed to Jimmy's financial support in college, Dr. Haisten likely sacrificed the most.

His income probably made him more affluent than the average person but not wealthy like the Hibbards. In relation to his personal wealth, he contributed a much greater percentage to Jimmy than did the Hibbards.

On 12 October 1960, only 4 months after Jimmy graduated from medical school, the doctor met a tragic death when preparing for a hunting trip. He reached into the closet for his shotgun and when he pulled it out by the barrel it accidentally went off, discharging a full load of lead shot point blank into his chest, killing him instantly.

He was only 56 years old. Recognizing the magnitude of what the doctor did for him, Jimmy considered him as second only to James Ballard among those who inspired him the most in life.

The best way Jimmy could think of honoring and memorializing him was to make Douglas the middle name of his son, Ballard when he was born.

Flush with a new infusion of funds, thanks to Dr. Douglas Haisten, Jimmy departed the Hibbards and Tuscaloosa at the end of his third pre-med year and found new lodging at Birmingham near the University Medical School to begin the final phase of becoming a physician.

Even though Birmingham's environment differed somewhat from that of Tuscaloosa, college life for Jimmy had become pretty much routine at that point in his educational journey. The smooth sailing encountered rough waters however, when an event occurred that risked leaving a stain on his otherwise spotless academic record.

While enrolled in his obstetrics course he and a group of students stood observing a senior resident in obstetrician training demonstrate the use of forceps in a delivery.

Noting that the resident had inserted the forceps upside down, which put the baby at risk, Jimmy advised him of the error and its potentially dire outcome.

Those words brought unmistakable hostility in the icy glare he fixed on Jimmy, but looking down at the instrument, he saw the error and immediately corrected it.

In acknowledging the grave risk to human life and welfare the error posed, a caring professional would have shown humility and gratitude for having the mistake pointed out to him, but not that individual. Instead, the resident gave Jimmy a flunking grade when the course ended. Jimmy described him as being from New Jersey with a view of southerners as vermin and himself personally as a redneck.

Professor Jones, head of the obstetrics department, called Jimmy in and asked him what happened. Instead of relating the incident and possibly destroying the resident's career, even though he had shown no concern for Jimmy's by flunking him, Jimmy responded to Professor Jones with no comment.

Sensing Jimmy's reluctance to tell him, the professor rightly guessed the problem not to be Jimmy's, but the person who failed him.

He resolved the matter by giving Jimmy another final exam which he easily passed, and changed his grade to an A, as it should have been in the first place.

That kept Jimmy's excellent record intact and word of his alert attention to details that saved a patient from possible harm got back to his University Hospital professors.

The obstetrician resident may or may not have suffered any negative consequences but the incident led to a positive outcome for Jimmy by bringing him to the attention of Dr. Ferguson, a professor of medicine at the University Hospital.

When it came time for Jimmy's 3-month externship Dr. Ferguson hired him to spend it working at the Baptist Hospital, a separate entity from the University Hospital.

And there, he met his soon to be wife, 24-year-old Martha Claire McGilvray, a direct 8th generation descendant of Creek Indian leader, Alexander McGillivray (1750-1793). A drop-dead gorgeous senior nursing student, in Jimmy's words, at the top of her class. He thought her the most beautiful thing he had ever seen and even better, she liked him too.

They spent their first few times together sitting across a coffee shop table from each other. Jimmy called them coffee shop dates because those were the only breaks they could spare from their busy schedules.

After about a month he got to know her pretty well and had begun to think they might have a future together. Then one day she walked into the hospital wearing an engagement ring.

That stunning development caught Jimmy completely off guard. During the time he had known her, she had said nothing about being involved with anybody else. Quite naturally puzzled, he asked her what happened.

She told him she had been dating this guy away at another college and during a recent visit home, he gave her the ring. Jimmy asked her how long she had dated him. She said off and on about 5 or 6 years. Jimmy thought, "crap!" he had been shot out of the saddle.

The news left him disconcerted, but he thought it wise not to say anything rash. The fiancé's name was Earp, a direct descendant of Wyatt Earp; famed marshal of wild-west lore. For about a month Jimmy remained indecisive as to what he should do, if anything.

That happened at the beginning of his junior year in 1958 and earlier in the year, he had received notice from the U. S. military informing him that induction into the service awaited him upon graduation.

Alternatively, the military had a program in which he could join the Air Force at the beginning of his senior year. He would receive the rank and pay of a Second Lieutenant and on graduating as an M. D., would be promoted to First Lieutenant.

He would then serve his 1-year internship in the military at the end of which he would be promoted to Captain and serve an additional 3 years in practice as an Air Force doctor.

Military service played no part in the future Jimmy had envisioned for himself. He felt betrayed by the government after spending 8 years of hard work in earning his medical degree.

The bitter edge of his disappointment dulled a little with the realization that joining the senior student program would end his chronic money problems, although not in the way he preferred.

Thinking that entering the program seemed the right thing if the draft awaited him regardless, he decided to go ahead and join up.

The idea began ruminating in the back of his mind that the military might not be so bad if he could persuade a certain senior nursing student to join him as an Air Force doctor's wife.

Bolstered by that hope, he decided to lay things on the line with Martha. He invited her to another coffee shop date. As he sat facing her across the table, he leaned close. Peering intently into her eyes, he told her he had a suggestion.

"What?" she asked. "You need to give that ring back to Wyatt," he told her. "Are you serious?" she asked, ignoring his sarcastic reference to her fiancé. "Deadly serious," he replied. She again asked why, and he told her, "Number 1, I know you, I like you, and I want our relationship to go wherever it might go, wherever that is and if you get married there is no way that can happen." Not following up with a number 2, he continued, "So, I think the fair thing is that you give the ring back to the guy." "OK," she said.

She gave it back and the wherever of the relationship found them before a preacher who married them 30 May 1959 at the Methodist Church her parents attended in Birmingham.

Her mother later confided to Jimmy that Martha had accepted the engagement ring from her former fiancé half-heartedly. Her uncertainty of their relationship left her cool to the idea but he pressured her into it, which explained why Jimmy so easily convinced her to return it.

Her parents were Wesley Varnado and Eddie Maude Hill McGilvray. They married 30 June 1933 in Jefferson County, Alabama. When Wesley registered for the WWII draft in October 1940, he identified his employer as Tennessee Coal Iron and Railroad Company.

The Company's employee hospital, by coincidence, employed Dr. Douglas Haisten during his internship from July 1928 to July 1929.

Wesley's brother, Sam McGilvray, (William Samuel McGilvray, 1908-1996) worked for Firestone Rubber Co., as Los Angeles District Manager for a time and remained an employee of the company for over 40 years.

Firestone had 5 divisions spread across the U. S. and Sam enjoyed the distinction as the only company executive to ever serve as the head of each of them during his career. When owner, Harvey S. Firestone died in 1938, Sam, who had been his personal assistant for many years, arranged to fly his casket from Miami Beach, Florida where he died, back home to Columbiana, Ohio, for burial.

Allegedly, Sam told the story that when the plane landed in Ohio, the heavy brass coffin weighed so much they had to call for a special ambulance to transport it. When he exited the plane and walked around the ambulance, Sam noticed its tires bore the name Good Year. On seeing that, he swore that Harvey Firestone would not take his last ride on Good Year tires. He proved it by calling the factory to send out a set of Firestones for mounting on the ambulance before it left the airport.

In another of his stories, Sam told of how Harvey Firestone along with Henry Ford, Thomas Edison and the naturalist and essayist, John Burroughs, were traveling together on a trip to south Florida in the 1920s.

When the model T Ford in which they rode had a head light go out, they stopped at a gas station somewhere in the boonies to get it fixed. As the mechanic at the station put a screwdriver to the light in removing the glass lens so he could replace the bulb, Sam, their driver, began telling him who the men riding in the car were.

Pointing at one of the men, he said that is Henry Ford, he built this car. Nodding at another, he said that is Thomas Edison over there, he built this light you are fixing. Next, he pointed to a stack of new tires for sale on display in front of the service station. My boss, Harvey Firestone made those he said, and that's him over there.

By that point the crusty old mechanic had about all he could stand of the big talk coming from who he thought to be just some young blow hard and motioning toward John Burroughs with his flowing snow-white beard, said sarcastically, "next I guess you are going to tell me he is Santa Clause."

Sam actually went to work for Firestone at a very early age, possibly as young as 16, and often served as his driver. As leaders in American industry at the time, those 4 men were known to be friends who often worked and vacationed together, calling themselves the "Vagabonds."

Sam probably embellished the story at least a little by including John Burroughs in it. He died in 1921 when Sam, born in 1908, was 13 years old. At that young age, it seems absurd that such important and supposedly responsible men would put him behind the wheel of a car being driven on public roads.

Sam may have become involved with Firestone in Miami because on the 1935 Florida state census for Miami-Dade County where he then resided, his listed his occupation as "college," presumably as a student rather than an employee.

The census gave his age as 26 and identified his wife's first name as Annalette. They married in Montgomery, Alabama in 1933 at his age of 24 and hers of 21. The marriage record identified her full name as Annulette Chandler. They married the same year as Martha's parents.

A year after he and Martha married, Jimmy received his M. D. diploma on graduation from medical school in June 1960. Along with his diploma came a promotion to Air Force 1st Lieutenant and orders to Tripler Army Medical

Center in Honolulu the following week where he would serve his one-year internship.

But before he left, his old friends and benefactors, the Hibbards, celebrated his graduation with a party to which they invited Jimmy's family and all his most special friends. They gave him a send-off he would never forget as he departed for Tripler to begin his career as a practicing physician.

The facility that would become Tripler Hospital originated in the 1907 turn of the century army post of Fort Shafter on the island of Oahu, when Hawaii remained a U. S. territory.

It later became the namesake of Civil War Union General Charles Stuart Tripler (1806-1866). The hospital as it appeared to Jimmy on his arrival there in 1960 had been completed in 1948. It stands on Moanalua Ridge overlooking Honolulu.

Administered by the U. S. Army, it is headquarters of the Pacific Regional Medical Command of the armed forces which serves the medical needs of all branches of the U. S. military in the region.

At Tripler, Jimmy learned the Air Force handled military personnel dependents differently than did the Army and Navy. When he sent for Martha to join him in Honolulu, he had to buy her a ticket on a commercial air carrier for transportation to Hawaii.

The other two services however, provided dependent transportation, along with shipment of household goods, free of charge. They also provided interns and their dependents free housing on base, which the Air Force did not.

To his good fortune, Jimmy arrived at a time when the Navy had unoccupied officer housing that they made available to him at no charge.

He viewed his circumstances as somewhat ironic in that as an Air Force intern he practiced in an Army hospital while residing in Navy housing.

It was only a few months after Jimmy arrived at Tripler that his friend and medical school sponsor, Dr. Douglas Haisten met his untimely death. His loss so overwhelmed his widow, Helen, with grief that she encountered health problems.

When Jimmy learned of her difficulties, he notified her she needed to be among friends and invited her to Hawaii as his and Martha's guest for as long as needed to regain her physical and emotional health.

She enjoyed their hospitality and generosity for an extended period of time which gave Jimmy the opportunity to repay, partially at least, the benevolence her late husband had bestowed on him.

She remained with them in 1961. Early one morning in March of that year, Jimmy rushed Martha to the hospital when she went into labor with their first child. Arriving at the hospital, he checked her into the obstetrics department.

About 4 hours later the nurse in whose care he left her came to Jimmy and told him the doctor scheduled to deliver the baby had not arrived. She further advised him the way things were going the baby might beat the doctor there.

Jimmy had delivered 7 babies since arriving at Tripler, and thinking he might have to deliver this one, began scrubbing and dressing in preparation.

About the time he had himself ready the tardy doctor walked in and asked what he intended to do.

He apprised him of the baby's imminent coming and his preparation for its delivery in the event no other doctor showed up on time

The doctor asked if he planned to deliver his own baby, to which Jimmy told him yeah, he started it and guessed he could finish it. The doctor laughed and told him he liked his attitude.

Taking charge of the delivery, the doctor very shortly presented Jimmy with his first baby girl, Penelope (Penny) Ancilia, born 29 March, 1961.

They did not have a bassinette for her so Martha lined a dresser drawer with a pillow to serve that purpose. On finishing his internship at Tripler, the following June 30, Jimmy received his promised promotion to Captain.

After Tripler he chose the School of Aerospace Medicine in San Antonio, Texas as his next post of duty. As he put it, the Air Force allowed him the choice as a way to make up for drafting him right out of medical school and depriving him of the much more professionally and financially rewarding practice in civilian medicine he looked forward to at the time.

In that spirit of generosity, the Air Force allowed him to pick his duty stations and specialty of choice the entire time of his service.

At the Aerospace Medicine School, he opted for the specialty of Flight Surgeon. As the name implies, his training focused on health issues specific to both commissioned and enlisted personnel assigned to aviation related duties and involved a great deal of flying himself.

On graduation from the Aerospace Medicine School in July 1961, he again took the discretion allowed him of selecting his own duty station.

He chose Eglin Air Force Base, Florida. Located in the panhandle about a hundred miles south-west of the Alabama farm where he grew up and where his parents still lived at the time; it put them close enough to exchange visits in a 2-hour drive.

At the time he and Martha settled into their new home off base near Eglin, Helen Haisten, who became their house guest back at Tripler in Honolulu, remained with them.

Jimmy accepted her extended stay with them as the least he could do to repay her for all she and her late husband, Dr. Haisten, had done for him during his time in pre-med at Tuscaloosa and medical school at U. A. B. He had no misgivings about helping her, because, in his mind, how could it not be the right thing to do.

He grew so fond of them at the time that he viewed them as a second set of parents, in addition to those to which he belonged biologically. Helen remained welcome in his home as long as she wanted to stay, but while at Eglin, she moved out after a new love came into her life and he asked for her hand in marriage. His name was Gillis Griffin, from Dothan.

Helen still owned the home she and Douglass had shared in Dothan, but decided to sell it after remarrying. Douglas and she married after his first wife, the mother of his four children, left him a widower.

When Helen put the house on the market, the Haisten children expressed no interest in the furnishings it contained although Helen invited them to take anything they wanted. They had a 90-day grace period allowed in the sales contract during which they could remove it if they changed their minds.

Jimmy knew that Dr. Haisten built replica antique furniture as a hobby. He specialized in the designs of English cabinet maker, George Hepplewhite (1727-1786), a contemporary of Thomas Chippendale, well known to collectors of fine antique English furniture.

Although Dr. Haisten built the furniture as a hobby, he did not turn out amateurish work. In his workshop equipped with every woodworking tool and machine imaginable, he crafted from Philippine mahogany beautiful pieces of work indistinguishable from the very best originals Hepplewhite ever made.

After the Haisten children turned down Helen's offer of the furniture, which they referred to as junk, she told Jimmy to look at the furnishings in the house and to take anything he wanted. Before the grace period ended, he decided to drive up to Dothan and take a look at the contents of the house.

When he found that it included many of Dr. Haisten's Hepplewhite replicas, it dumbfounded him that no one in the family wanted them. Thinking them too valuable to give away, he decided to put them somewhere for safekeeping in the event Helen changed her mind.

The best place he could think of to store them was an old barn on his dad's place that had long been empty. Driving down to Rehobeth, he borrowed Arthur's pickup, hauled the furniture to the farm and unloaded it in the barn. It took him 5 trips to move it all.

Before departing, he spread old burlap bags over the furniture to protect it to the extent possible from dust, trash, bird droppings, and anything else landing on it over time that might leave a stubborn to remove flaw in the finish.

And just as Jimmy feared, the time came when Helen regretted letting the furniture go with the house. Not telling her what he did, he invited her on a visit with him to the farm. When they walked into the barn and Jimmy threw off the croaker sacks to reveal the furniture, she burst into tears of happiness.

From her reaction on seeing the furniture, Jimmy knew he had done the right thing by saving it for her. It made her happy that he saved the furniture, but she later decided she had no room for all of it in her home and invited Jimmy to take any of it he wanted.

He accepted it and now has it in his house at the farm, to where it came many years after he assumed his duties as flight surgeon at Eglin.

A major role of Eglin's mission involved various aspects of air crew training which gave them much time in the air. Their missions took them over a wide area of the southeast U. S., the Gulf of Mexico and the Panama Canal Zone.

Jimmy recalled an incident in the Canal Zone when local police arrested a flight crew member in a barroom fight. Having learned to speak Spanish in pre-med school, Jimmy persuaded the police chief to release the airman so he could fly back home with the crew when they departed the area. If they had held him, he would have been AWOL putting him in trouble with the Air Force.

The flights Jimmy crewed regularly took them to the Canal Zone on training missions, and on the return trip from one of them, 1 of the 2 engines of their DC-3 quit.

The pilot somewhat allayed Jimmy's anxiety that they were going to crash into the Gulf of Mexico over which they flew by his assurance that they could easily make it home on one engine.

Jimmy's relief proved only temporary however, because when they were 3 hours out from Eglin, they flew into a fog bank so dense the airplane windshield looked like a TV screen showing nothing but white static.

The zero visibility presented no problems for the pilot because he could fly the plane on instruments. But when he radioed the Eglin control tower of their imminent approach and landing, they advised him the fog obscured runway would prevent him from landing under visual flight rules necessitating their verbal guidance in getting them down.

Jimmy's anxiety level shot even higher than before as the thought flashed through his mind that no way could they avoid finally crashing. In telling the story he became so emotional in his recollection of it that his voice broke and tears welled in his eyes as if he relived the experience all over again.

Although the next few agonizing minutes seemed to drag on endlessly as he listened to the back-and-forth chatter between the pilot and control tower, he soon found himself safely on the ground.

In those fearful moments he gained profound appreciation and respect for the courage and professional competence of the men who piloted the aircraft of the U. S. Air Force.

Flying blind and on 1 engine, the pilot of the DC-3 sat the plane's tires on the runway with barely a whisper under guidance of the control tower talking him down over the radio.

The pilot, Colonel Bill Page, had taken Jimmy aloft many times before, including in the back seat of his supersonic F-102 jet fighter.

The Colonel enjoyed demonstrating the plane's capabilities to Jimmy. On one occasion, he taxied out onto the extra-long B-52 bomber runway. He locked the brakes and pushed the engine to full throttle letting it rise to maximum thrust in a deafening, vibrating roar.

The instant he released the brakes the plane shot down the runway as if fired out of a cannon with the Colonel pushing the stick forward to keep it earth bound while gaining momentum. As the end of the runway loomed, he hauled back on the stick turning the nose of the plane vertical and within seconds, leveled off at 50 thousand feet.

Telling Jimmy to watch his seat belts, the Colonel put the plane into a weightless simulation maneuver. Jimmy's barely slack shoulder belts grew taut, restraining him from rising into the air as if liberated from gravity.

He felt himself floating above his seat instead of sitting on it. Everything about that flight greatly impressed him, but he had seen nothing yet.

That would come on the return leg of a training flight Jimmy took with Colonel Page to New Orleans in the fighter. The plane had been equipped with wing tanks to provide sufficient fuel for the flight which extended beyond its normal range.

On the way back the Colonel told Jimmy he needed to burn off the fuel in the wing tanks so he bumped the throttle up to a cruising speed near mach 3, or 3 times the speed of sound, which exceeded 2 thousand miles per hour.

They arrived at Eglin, landed, exited the plane and were walking toward the hangar when the Colonel laid his hand on Jimmy's arm and told him to listen, he was about to hear them getting there.

Momentarily, they heard the sonic boom of the plane breaking the sound barrier which it had done several minutes before they landed. It was a phenomenon of aeronautical physics so rare that it is known to only a select few people.

Although a secret at the time, an airstrip at Eglin was where pilots of General James Doolittle's raid over Tokyo,

Japan in WWII, trained to get their B-25 bombers air born short of the length of an air craft carrier's deck.

After training, the bombers were loaded on the carrier USS Hornet and transported across the Pacific Ocean to a point from which they could fly to the Japanese mainland and launched the morning of 18 April 1942.

They did minimal damage to Japan but news of the raid raised American morale and exposed the vulnerability of the Japanese homeland to attack. None of the 16 planes participating in the raid survived but more than 60 of the 80 airmen did.

A B-25 bomber similar to those in the mission is on display at Eglin as a memorial to General Doolittle's raid. In 1944 a movie based on the event came out. Titled "Thirty Seconds Over Tokyo," it starred Spencer Tracy and Van Johnson.

Jimmy himself became a star of sorts in the January 1964 edition of the "Airman" magazine. It featured an article about a helicopter rescue from a fishing boat in the Gulf:

> . . . A short time later, Captain Luttrell answered another distress call, this time from the *Early Bird*, a fishing boat. Waiting just long enough to refuel and pick up Dr. (Capt.) Jimmy Sheppard of Eglin's USAF Hospital, Captain Luttrell soon had the helicopter hovering over the boat to pick up an ailing Navy Petty Officer. Within an hour the mission was over and the patient was resting comfortably in the Eglin hospital. Diagnosis? Seasickness.

Jimmy recalled going along on the rescue because when the boat skipper made the distress call, he stated the sick man had blood in his vomit. On being lowered to the boat deck from the helicopter Jimmy examined the man and questioned him.

He said before he vomited, he was heaving and retching violently. From that, Jimmy concluded the bleeding came from burst blood vessels in the esophagus, rather than something more serious.

He put the man in the basket for hoisting up to the helicopter. The basket came back down to take Jimmy up and they transported the patient to the Eglin hospital.

As a doctor, Jimmy had the unpleasant duty on occasion to help clean up human remains in the aftermath of fatal accidents involving aircraft or ordinances they delivered.

He recalled an accident that involved a fighter jet practicing bombing runs with a fake bomb under the observation of 2 judges in a bunker. A hole in the ground topped with a roof, the bunker had an open viewing port about 2 feet high through which the observers could watch how closely the bomb came to the target.

Instead of sighting in on the designated target, the pilot erroneously targeted the bunker and the fake bomb flew straight through the viewing port.

It contained no explosives but the force of its kinetic energy on impact disintegrated both itself and the 2 occupants of the bunker. All that could be found of their remains were their hands, fingers and ears.

Another accident involved an F-105 fighter jet that dove straight into the ground at full throttle, burying the engine 12 feet deep on impact. Investigators speculated the pilot had passed out before the crash. Very little of his body could be found.

The Air Force gave Jimmy the opportunity to gain a great deal of experience and knowledge as an M. D., but more in the area of a general practitioner than in any particular specialty.

For that reason, he had no intention of making the Air Force his career even though he entertained reenlistment spiels from those with the job of persuading him to stay.

Well before his 4 years in the service ended, he began making plans to apply to the University of Florida medical school in Gainesville for a residency in internal medicine and cardiology.

Knowing that residents receive only a meager stipend, his plans included how he would support himself and his family during his 3-year residency.

He would do that by establishing a Volkswagen dealership in Andalusia, Alabama, that he believed would provide him with sufficient income. In researching Volkswagen dealership requirements, he learned the distance between dealerships could be no less than 40 miles.

Andalusia met that criterion, with the nearest dealership then in Troy, 45 miles away. Settling on that location, he hopped an Eglin mission flight to New Orleans, Louisiana.

He rented a car and drove to the International Auto Sales and Service organization, the distributor of Volkswagens sold in Louisiana, Mississippi, Alabama and Florida.

The cars were only manufactured in Germany then and ethnic German employees of the company controlled their distribution in the U. S. Those were the people Jimmy found himself dealing with.

He met with them and presented his proposal. They said they would do a market survey and get back to him. Within a short period of time, they notified him they had completed the survey and found Andalusia acceptable for a dealership.

They recommended he find a piece of property for the site and they would provide him with plans for the building. When he received the plans, the estimated cost of a quarter million dollars exceeded by 100 thousand dollars what he thought it should be.

Digging into the reason for the additional cost, he learned Volkswagen's dealership building plans were all identical in providing for snow load requirements, which accounted for the higher price. He told them no snow of more than a couple of inches had fallen in south Alabama in recorded history.

When they told him no matter; their policy permitted no changes in building design, he told them they could either allow the changes or he would walk away from the project. Apparently anticipating the new dealership more than their arrogance allowed them to show, they relented to the changes.

The Germans further required full-time on-site management by a person holding an ownership interest in the business. As an active Air Force officer, military regulations would not allow Jimmy to fill the spot himself.

It just so happened he had a colonel friend retiring from the service at the time and needed to occupy himself in post Air Force life. Jimmy brought him in as co-owner to comply with the management requirements, but kept the controlling interest of 51% for himself.

With the revised building plans and site costs in hand, and Volkswagen's favorable market survey as sweetener, Jimmy went to the bank and easily obtained the loan he needed to fund the project. The contractors went to work and soon had the facility ready for its grand opening. They named it "McNeese Motors," after Jimmy's colonel friend and co-owner.

The Germans would not allow Jimmy to give it his name because under their rules, it could only be named after a member of the on-site owner-manager team, for which only Colonel McNeese qualified. Following the employment of a sales staff, they filled the lot with shiny new Volkswagens for them to sell.

The cars sold like hot cakes from the beginning, especially the popular and inexpensive Beetle which became ubiquitous on American highways in the 1960s and for decades afterwards. Things went so well that everybody, except the Germans, it seemed, were happy.

Trouble brewed between them and the dealership over radios being installed in the cars. The Germans had mandated installation of only their model of radios in vehicles the dealership sold.

The dealership on the other hand, had an American model both they and the customers preferred and it sold for less than the German radio. Ignoring the Germans, the dealership went happily along putting the American radio in customers' new cars.

One day a gentleman with a strong German accent walked into the manager's office and introduced himself as a representative of the VW regional distributor.

In an arrogantly authoritative tone, he told the manager he would install only the German radio in cars the dealership received from the regional distributor in the future. Management thanked him for coming and bade him goodbye on his way out.

After he left, they kept using the American radios until the dealership's next shipment of new cars became overdue. They called the regional distributor to find out why and were told they would receive the cars with their next order of German radios. Needless to say, from that point forward, the German radio became their standard installation.

By the time Jimmy's term of service in the Air Force ended in 1964 the dealership had begun generating the income he needed to live on while he spent his 3-year residency at the University of Florida School of Medicine.

As soon as his discharge from the Air Force became effective, he moved his family, which had grown the previous year with the birth of Pamela Marie on 6 March 1963, to Gainesville to begin his residency.

He joined several other residents at the medical school, each of whom represented the internal medicine sub-specialties of cardiology, pulmonology, nephrology (renal medicine), dermatology, neurology, and Gastro-enterology.

During their residency they rotated through each of the subspecialty areas. In other words, they all spent a period of time working as teams in each area.

Dr. Robert Cade headed the school's renal medicine department as professor. The other residents with whom Jimmy teamed were Dr. Howard Ramsey, a Dr. Sealman (spelling uncertain) and he could not recall the third name. One afternoon during their renal medicine rotation the 4 residents were in the renal department working with artificial kidney patients on dialysis when the football coach came in wanting to talk to Dr. Cade.

On being advised of Dr. Cades absence at the time, the coach told Jimmy and his fellow residents the players were passing out in the hot weather during football practice. He said they were drinking plenty of ice water but it helped very little.

The residents told him the players were passing out because they were not replacing the minerals lost in their heavy sweating. The coach asked what could be done about that and the doctors told him he could just put minerals in their water. "I am desperate," the coach told them. "Can you help me out?" he wanted to know.

Just looking at each other like they viewed it as such a simple thing to solve, the doctors told him they could mix up something and let him try it.

They sterilized one of the big stainless-steel vats they used in renal medicine and filled it with a 20-gallon mixture of water and minerals. The minerals were those contained in perspiration, including sodium, potassium chloride and others the players were losing in sweat. They added a couple gallons of orange juice to improve the taste and gave it to the coach.

About 10 days later the coach came back and told the residents the players were drinking the mineral water and were no longer passing out, but thought it could taste better. The doctors told him they would add a little more orange juice to make it sweeter.

That made it more palatable but the coach came back later saying the players thought the taste still needed work. "Do you know what they are calling it?" he asked the doctors. They said no, and he told them "Gatorade."

Jimmy thought that happened about 1966 but could not remember for sure. After he completed his residency and left the medical school, he heard nothing else about Gatorade until a soft drink company, he couldn't remember which one, contacted him several years later wanting to buy his rights to it. The company, he said, offered him a million dollars for his share, but he declined it.

Technically, as an employee of the University at the time, the University legally owned anything created or invented by its employees. He feared that if he accepted the offer, he would end up in a legal fight over it with the University, which he had no desire to do.

According to numerous newspaper articles on Gatorade, its development began in 1965 under the leadership of Dr. Robert Cade when the Gator football coach sought help in solving the problem of football players becoming severely dehydrated in the hot weather during football practice.

The doctors working with Dr. Cade included Dana Shire, H. James Free and Alejandro de Quesada. Dr. Cade is credited as the inventor of Gatorade. The team likely included other unidentified individuals who worked on the project.

Jimmy and his fellow residents were among them, but they considered the work they did on Gatorade as peripheral to their residencies and received no recognition in any media reporting on it.

Improving the taste and naming it Gatorade actually came later than Jimmy recalled. Dr. Cade established the first company to sell the sports drink, which he dubbed The Gatorade Company, Inc. In 1967, he sold Stokley-Van Camp the rights to produce and market it.

The University at first showed little interest in it until the big money began rolling in. Then, just as Jimmy feared, they sued for the rights based on the use of university employees and facilities in developing it. But they settled with Cade when he agreed to share royalties with the University.

Quaker Oats purchased the brand in 1983 and sold it to PepsiCo in 2000. Cade and his 3 doctors credited with the research and development became wealthy and the University at last count had earned over 100 million from its share of the royalties. The product is marketed world-wide and has made billions of dollars in sales.

Jimmy recalled that he and his fellow residents viewed the work they did on Gatorade in 1965 as trivial because they spent so little time on it.

Besides, Polly Anna, his third child, arrived on 8 December that year at the University School of Medicine Hospital giving him more important things to think about.

By the time he completed his residency in 1967 he had pretty much forgotten about Gatorade and looked forward to beginning his internal medicine and cardiology practice in Ft. Walton Beach.

III

≈MEDICAL PRACTICE≈

In
Ft. Walton Beach, Buying the Farm, Building the
House, a Son's Birth and a Death in the Family.

On returning to Ft. Walton Beach from Gainesville
in 1967, Jimmy began his medical practice at the Magnolia
Clinic operated by general practitioners, Doctors Robert
Maxon and Bernard Russell.

About 6 months later he sold the Volkswagen dealership. As he put it, he made a bundle when he owned the
business and made another bundle when he sold it.

It had served him far beyond expectations in providing his financial support during the 3 years of his specialist
residency. As with most important decisions he had made
up to that point, the success of the dealership proved, yet
again, that he had chosen well in the paths he took.

As the first specialist in cardiology and internal medicine in Ft. Walton Beach, the White-Wilson Medical Center
heavily recruited him but he opted for Magnolia instead.
Doctors Maxon and Russell were generally regarded as good

practitioners and Jimmy believed associating with them would enhance his own standing in the medical community.

Dr. Cyrus Guynn, who went through residency with Jimmy at the University of Florida School of Medicine, later came to Magnolia and partnered with him in his practice.

A diabetic female became one of Jimmy's earliest patients. Pronounced DOA on arrival at the emergency room, she had no pulse, heartbeat or other signs of life. Emergency room doctors began resuscitating her under Jimmy's supervision and re-established her vital signs.

When treated with insulin, she recovered from the diabetic coma she had lapsed into. That happened, Jimmy learned in discussions with her afterwards, because she had not been following an appropriate diabetic diet and insulin regimen.

She had been ignoring her diabetes and basically eating herself to death. Perhaps scared into it by her near-death encounter, she began taking better care of herself and lived more than 20 years after that.

Jimmy believed his success with that case helped his practice immensely. With his specialist training he had the skills to do a lot of things a general practitioner could not.

After remaining at Magnolia for 5 years Jimmy decided he wanted to establish his own clinic in which he could limit his practice exclusively to internal medicine and cardiology. When he informed Dr. Russell of that, the doctor threatened to sue him if he left Magnolia.

For the purpose of mediating the dispute out of court, Russell's attorney asked both plaintiff and defendant to meet with him in his office.

When the attorney inquired of his reason for suing, Dr. Russell replied that Jimmy's wanting to leave Magnolia clinic angered him. The attorney told him being mad did not justify suing anybody.

He asked Jimmy why he wanted to leave and Jimmy told him that in working with general practitioners, much of his work involved patient care unrelated to his specialties of cardiology and internal medicine.

More often than not, his work involved patients in need of pediatric, gynecological or obstetrical care, which were not specialties in which he had trained. The same applied to much of the care he provided to patients coming into the emergency room.

He felt that the time he spent in those areas caused his specialist training to languish, contrary to what should be happening if he hoped to continue in those types of medical practice.

He preferred to practice those specialties exclusively and needed to establish his own clinic to do that.

The attorney managed to convince Dr. Russell he had no grounds for a suit and he agreed to drop it.

The mediation eliminated the threatened law suit, freeing Jimmy to leave Magnolia and proceed with his clinic plans. He built it on 2 acres at a Beal Parkway address he acquired one block south of the Mary Esther Cut Off. It included a cardiovascular clinic that enabled them to provide similar cardiology services available to patients at the hospital.

The first of its kind in Florida, it included a cardiology evaluation unit equipped for outpatient treadmill stress testing, echo cardiograms, EKGs, chest X rays and other related tests.

Dr. Curtis Williams, one of the doctors in residency with Jimmy at the University of Florida, had gone into practice in Pensacola. He came over and looked at Jimmy's facility for guidance in designing and equipping a similar clinic for his own practice.

A service that Jimmy's clinic could not provide that the Ft. Walton hospital could was surgery. He and his partner were strictly noninvasive cardiologists. They did not get into Swan-Ganz – right heart catheterizations, atherectomies and other such invasive treatments

Jimmy's role in treating those and other disorders involved identifying symptoms, performing tests and evaluations, then diagnosing and recommending the appropriate surgical procedures.

Following that he turned his patients and their workups over to surgeons at the hospital to handle the invasive aspects of the treatments.

On occasion, Jimmy consulted with other doctors in treating their patients. Dr. White of White-Wilson clinic called him in on one such case involving the mysterious malady a patient of his suffered.

Dr. White phoned at 11:00 p. m., telling him the patient's ailment defied diagnosis. Describing her prognosis as dire without something being done soon to help her, he asked Jimmy to go over and examine her, to which he agreed.

On arrival he learned the patient had been unconscious for 2 days. He found her cyanotic with a weak heartbeat as he leaned over her with his stethoscope.

As he stood listening, his eyes fell aimlessly on the oxygen control box through which the tube to her oxygen mask passed and what he saw brought both alarm and relief.

It alarmed him that the control box lid pinched the tube, blocking the flow to the patient's oxygen mask. The oxygen mask in turn covered both her mouth and nose, preventing her from breathing ambient air.

That explained both the patient's cyanosis and weak heart rate. He felt relieved that he arrived in time to save her from suffocation, with which he diagnosed her.

He extricated the pinched tube and turned the oxygen control higher, from 5 to 6 liters. Momentarily, he detected a strengthening heartbeat and noted fading of the cyanosis as her skin color returned to normal. Within minutes she regained consciousness and seemed well on her way to recovery.

He told Dr. White the patient showed significant improvement and would probably be ok. Further, he thought they were doing all the right things for her. He never disclosed to Dr. White the nature of the real problem.

That case came with the lesson that a life-saving treatment can sometimes be nothing more than the correction of a careless, though dangerous, mechanical error.

In other instances, a successful treatment might be as simple as suggesting a change in life style. Jimmy used that approach on the smoking habit of his father who became his patient after he started practicing at Ft. Walton Beach.

Arthur still smoked at the time, although sparingly. A Surgeon General's report on the harmful effects of smoking had recently come out that alarmed Jimmy.

Prompted by the report, when Arthur came in for his second annual checkup, Jimmy decided to try encouraging him to give up cigarettes.

He told him about the Surgeon General's report, but Arthur, ever the one to come up with a well-reasoned argument, told him that according to his brother G. W., during World War II the government gave soldiers little miniature packs of cigarettes as a treat. If the government gave them out free, he asked, how could they be dangerous?

Jimmy replied it had been recently determined that smoking caused a number of health issues, including emphysema, heart disease, strokes, and heart attacks. Once they start, even if smoking is stopped, these conditions generally worsen with age.

Jimmy told him he knew he didn't smoke a lot, but the Surgeon General's report raised his concerns. You really need to stop, Jimmy told him, and the reason is that it is important to you.

Jimmy continued, saying he had a responsibility to be insistent on matters important to the health of his patients, to which Arthur replied that he would think seriously about it.

On his way out of the office Arthur stopped by the desk of Jimmy's receptionist Mary Jane, and asked her if she had Buddy's phone number. Mary Jane asked why he needed it, to which he replied he wanted a second opinion.

Buddy, aka Jimmy's younger brother, Dr. Arthur Robert, subsequently became a professor at UAB medical school.

Buddy filled Jimmy in later. He said Arthur showed up at his office about 2 weeks after that. He began asking questions about smoking and Buddy told him the same thing Jimmy had. He asked if he agreed with Jimmy and Buddy told him he did and gladly, Jimmy made an issue of it.

When Arthur got back home, he pulled the pack of cigarettes out of his shirt pocket and laid them on the mantle. "That finishes that," Lola later told Jimmy he said. He never smoked another cigarette.

In spite of quitting cigarettes, Arthur became asthmatic in his 50s. Jimmy thought dust at the fertilizer plant caused it rather than smoking.

Wheezing and shortness of breath increasingly troubled him as the condition gradually worsened in the contaminated air at work. He suffered with it for about 30 years and it eventually became so severe that Jimmy asked him how he had continued working for so long under those conditions.

Arthur told him the local general practitioner had been giving him shots every 2 weeks to control it.

Jimmy called the doctor regarding the shots and learned they were steroids. That concerned him because he knew steroids were contraindicated for long-term use.

They caused thinning of the bones, peptic ulcers, high blood pressure, diabetes and other problems worse than asthma.

It might be assumed that disorders like those would shorten a person's life, but Arthur defied any such expectations by living to the age of 82 (18 Nov. 1912-12 Mar. 1995), even more remarkable, considering the average life expectancy then spanned only 75.62 years. When he died, his death record listed asthma as a contributing cause.

At some point during the time Jimmy served as his father's physician, the last person in the world he ever expected to grace his clinic walked in. None other than Bob Hope, possibly the world's best-known entertainer at the time, came in complaining of chest discomfort.

Visiting the area in connection with a charity he supported and sponsored, the Air Force Colonel acting as his liaison with the Air Force, himself a patient of Jimmy's, brought him to the clinic.

Jimmy examined him and gave him a cardiogram, but found nothing indicating a serious problem wrong with him. He recommended however, that Hope undergo a thorough examination by his regular doctor.

Hope visited Jimmy's clinic several times after that, but for social rather than medical reasons. Jimmy recalled that Hope kidded one of his nurses with an odd name, asking her how such a pretty woman ended up with a name like that. He phrased it in a way that had the nurse and everyone else in the clinic laughing in stitches.

He had come to the area in support of the Air Force Enlisted Village program in nearby Shalimar. The idea for the AFEV as it is sometime called, originated in 1967 when a group of active-duty and retired Air Force noncommissioned officers, got together to do something for the destitute widows of deceased enlisted airmen.

The meager retirement benefits these airmen received after retiring from a career in the Air Force barely ever provided them with sufficient income in post-retirement on which to live without other employment to supplement the retirement benefits.

In many instances, they died without having vested in the retirement programs of the other employment, assuming one existed in the first place, which they often did not, leaving their widows with no income but the poverty level Air Force retirement benefits.

The AFEV foundation, a 501(c) (3) not for profit charity, grew out of efforts to address the paltry resources of those women to live on by making available to them low-income housing they could afford.

Bob Hope, recognized as one of the most notable benefactors of the AFEV, performed many times at the villages to help raise funds needed in their support. At last count, 6 of the villages had been established in Bob Hope's name and housed some 500 residents in independent living apartments.

The AFEV came to Ft. Walton in 1967, the same year Jimmy began his practice there. In the early years the town remained the place of his residence because of its convenience to his practice but he looked forward to the time he could find a place to live more to his liking.

By the end of the 1960s, he and Martha had the 3 girls, Penny, Pam and Polly; the "3 Ps," they called them and after 8 years of living in an overcrowded small-town, Jimmy had grown weary of the traffic, pollution, tourists and noise.

In winter the snowbirds crowded the streets and restaurants, turning parking and finding a place to eat without a long wait, into a nightmare. When the snowbirds moved out with the coming of summer, the beach crowds from Alabama, Georgia and other parts of Florida, moved in.

The only noticeable change came in the accents of the tourists and — some might say — the color of their necks. Otherwise, they numbered no less than the snowbirds and the streets and restaurants became no less a nightmare.

All of it finally becoming more than he could stand, Jimmy told Martha he had enough and wanted to find a better place to live. She said OK and he began what would be a 2-year search before he found what he sought.

One day when driving the back roads in his search, the direction of his travel took him from the southeast corner of Walton County back toward DeFuniak Springs.

Although actually lost, he had a good idea in general, of his approximate location. Heading north on McKinnon Bridge Road, he passed what appeared to be a vacant farm house on the left as he approached Bruce Creek Bridge, a short distance ahead.

Something about the place piquing his interest, he turned around, drove back to the house and pulled into the driveway. A dirt lane continued from the driveway down a hill through some woods further into the property.

Getting out of the car he walked down the lane to where it joined a large field overgrown with weeds. As he looked across the field and into the woods fringing it, and Bruce Creek beyond, his eyes presented him with one of the most tranquil and pleasing views of natural scenery he could have imagined. He wanted a place with scenic beauty, water and big trees and he knew he had found it.

He got back in his car and drove on to the courthouse in DeFuniak Springs to look up the owner of the property in the county deed records. Finding her name, he phoned her about buying it, but she told him she did not want to sell it.

He told her he understood, but he thought it a pretty piece of property and if she ever changed her mind to please let him know. As he recalled that was about 1973.

Another 8 months or so, passed without hearing from her. Then, sometime around June 1974, she called him back inquiring if he still wanted to buy the property. He told her yes and offered a down payment with the balance to be paid off in 3 years, to which she agreed.

The warranty deed she gave him for the 160 acres on 18 July 1974 identified her as Mary Destin Nicholson. She eventually became one of his patients and remained under his care until her death a number of years later.

Spurred on by his preference for a sooner rather than later change of address from Ft. Walton Beach, Jimmy began making preparations to move to the farm.

He took Martha and the children out for a look and they loved it, especially the children. They planned on moving into the existing house, which, although structurally sound, needed the electrical and plumbing systems modernized.

As the renovation work on the vintage home proceeded and they made frequent trips between the farm and Ft. Walton, the 55-mile one-way drive began impressing on Martha the remoteness of the farm from the city, giving her second thoughts about the move.

When she voiced her concerns to Jimmy, he told her that if she didn't think she would be happy out there, they wouldn't move.

The girls however, did not share her doubts. The prospect of having horses and other animals and such a large place to roam and explore had them all excited. Not moving would be a major disappointment to them.

Preferring not to impose his opinion on the rest of the family, Jimmy felt it best for Martha and the girls to talk it over and whatever they agreed on, the family would do.

That seemed satisfactory to Martha and the girls. In the end however, Martha may have regretted agreeing to it because the girls were of the mind that moving to the farm would be good for everybody.

As later events would show, Martha never really cared for the farm, but she relented to the move, because, in Jimmy's words, she wanted to do what the girls wanted.

As his first building project after moving into the renovated farm house, Jimmy began the biggest of his barns that would house his future antique tractor collection, which at the time his plans for the farm did not include. He finished the barn in 1975 and began construction on a new house the next year, completing it within that space of time.

Jimmy purchased the cypress lumber sheathing the exterior walls of both the barn and house from a lumber mill in Caryville, located in Holmes County on the east bank of the Choctawhatchee River.

He chose cypress, first; for its natural durability against rot and insect damage, and second; for the beautiful grey patina it acquires with age, enabling it to blend softly into its forested surroundings rather than standing in stark contrast to them, as bricks would.

As a possible third reason, it reflected his sentimentality for the rustic farm houses he so warmly remembered from a poor, but mostly happy, childhood.

When Jimmy acquired the cypress lumber for his barn, house and separate garage, he anticipated its use in future buildings. Accordingly, he ordered 50 thousand board feet and stored that in excess of his immediate needs in the loft of the big barn after he finished building it.

The completed barn gave him plenty of space to house the tractors, equipment, materials and supplies he thought he would need in operating the farm he hoped to establish.

As he began developing the property, he cleared the field of the weeds choking it when he first arrived, and put in Argentine Bahia grass. That resulted in an island of grass several dozen acres in size surrounded by thick forests of mixed hardwoods with a smattering of pines, cedar and juniper.

He set the buildings back in the fringes of the woods so as to make them less conspicuous than if they stood in the open meadow. As intended, the weathered cypress on the buildings gave them low visibility among the trees.

The red front door of the 7 thousand square foot, 2 story house opens to the meadow and its back deck sits only a few feet from the edge of a 30-foot-high vertical bluff overlooking a bend in Bruce Creek.

A couple of years before they moved to the farm, Martha informed Jimmy she would like to have another child, preferably a son, since they already had the 3 girls. Jimmy, on the other hand, had his doubts about the idea because he felt she had her wagon overloaded with the girls being 2 years apart and having another child seemed imprudent to him.

Martha argued that she had managed quite well with the girls. She had learned a lot about child raising with them, and felt she would have no problems with another child.

Finally, after they had moved to the farm and built the new house, Jimmy told her they would have another child if she would have tests done during the pregnancy to determine if the baby was normal, and if it was not, she would terminate the pregnancy, and they would try again.

They were both 41 years old at the time and knew that babies born to women in that age range had a greater risk of genetic abnormalities. She told him "OK," she would have the tests done and they could decide what to do based on the results.

She became pregnant about February 1977, and as agreed to, she had amniocentesis and sonograms done. The results indicated not only that the baby seemed normal, but also, that they would soon be welcoming a son. She could not have been more ecstatic on hearing all the good news she had hoped for.

The pregnancy came to term without incident and baby Ballard Douglas Sheppard arrived on 11 October, 1977, at the hospital in Ft. Walton Beach. His birth came just one day short of the 17th anniversary of the death of Dr. Douglas Haisten, for whom Jimmy gave Ballard his second name.

As Jimmy put it, the child's mother spoiled him something rotten. He became a juvenile delinquent by the age of one. She catered to him, waited on him and spoiled him until he became worthless. Jimmy tried talking to her about the way she mothered him.

He told her she didn't do that with the girls, and the kid would grow up to be impossible. She told him, no, she wasn't spoiling him, and proceeded to do just that in Jimmy's view.

Within a few years after Ballard's birth, Martha began experiencing symptoms of menopause. As Jimmy put it, she had a whole personality change and he didn't want to be in the same county with her. She became suspicious, cynical and condescending. She didn't like him and he didn't like her, which led them to make separate living arrangements.

But the decision to live apart involved more than just the alienation of their relationship. Having grown up a city girl, Martha never liked living on the farm because she found it not only too far from city life, but threatening as well. The wildlife seemed everywhere; alligators in the creek, bobcats roaming about, and the occasional black bear or Florida panther passing through.

To give her respite from the farm as she wanted or needed, they bought a little townhouse down at Swift Bayou in Niceville in the time frame of 1986-88. She and Ballard stayed there much of the time and Jimmy on the farm. She could not have been happier with the arrangement and they made it work that way.

Martha worked a number of years after Ballard came along. She told Jimmy she needed to work just to have something to do. Even though a registered nurse by education and training, she did not always work in that profession. She worked for a time at a Ft. Walton ladies apparel shop until it went out of business.

When Dr. Cyrus Guynn ended his partnership with Jimmy at the clinic to move back to his home state of Virginia for family reasons, Dr. Jim Wilson replaced him as Jimmy's partner. He hired Martha as his nurse for a time during which she and Jimmy had to appear to get along for the benefit of the practice and marriage.

Martha worked for Dr. Wilson until an issue arose that led him to terminate her employment. She then persuaded Jimmy to give her a job as his nurse on the condition they would try it for 90 days to see how it went.

Again, for the sake of the practice, they made it work in spite of a few differences over clinic staff. Martha demanded Jimmy fire the young woman he employed as his lab. Tech. and he refused to do so. In his mind, the woman performed her job well and he had no reason for terminating her.

Martha wanted her fired because she refused to take orders from her, something the woman had no obligation to do because she worked for Jimmy; not Martha.

In her role as a nurse, Martha treated patients professionally in a friendly and considerate manner, so much so that she often earned their affection. Some found her so captivating as to call her "angelic." Jimmy praised her for that, but it dismayed him that she had a better relationship with the patients than with him.

In 1993, at age 60, Martha learned she had cancer. Her gynecologist found the little tumor when doing her annual checkup. Diagnosed as leiomyosarcoma of the uterus, an odd, rare, vicious cancer, it had given her no symptoms whatsoever.

It took a couple of different pathologists to confirm it as leiomyosarcoma because of its extreme infrequency. Her doctor told Martha it had an 88 to 94 percent fatality rate. In view of that chilling prognosis, no time could be spared in getting her the best possible treatment.

Her doctors referred her to the Alabama School of Medicine, Department of Gynecology, in Birmingham for radical "clean out" surgery, as the first step in her treatment. That involved the excision of all her internal female organs susceptible to the malignancy.

Additionally, her doctors recommended she undergo both chemo and radiation treatments as adjunctive therapy to the surgery.

As the most highly recommended place she could go for the therapy, her doctors referred her to the Carolinas Medical Center Hospital in Charlotte, North Carolina. It had diagnosed and treated more cases of that particular type cancer than any other clinic in the United States.

Before agreeing to the therapy, she asked Jimmy what he would do if he were her. That question he had prayed she would never ask, because he knew as a doctor, he would have to tell her what he feared the truth to be.

He told her that if in her place, he would do nothing else because he suspected that when they did the radical surgery, they either cured her, or she would never be cured. As a health care professional herself, Martha recognized at some level the truth of what Jimmy told her.

But knowing she suffered a potentially lethal disease had no doubt left her in an emotionally fragile state. What she needed more than anything else at that point was not the emotionally detached cold hard truth of a doctor's opinion, but the comforting words of a caring and sympathetic husband who might offer her the glimmer of hope that she so desperately sought and needed. As Jimmy recalled, the conversation ended with Martha in tears.

He did not divulge how he felt at the time because he viewed the exchange between them as an intensely personal and private matter. Martha seems to have felt the same way as she refused to share the details with her daughter, Penny, on whom she depended and trusted the most during the final years and months of her life.

Finally deciding on her own to go ahead with the therapy, she drove to the North Carolina hospital once a month to receive the treatments. Jimmy tried persuading her to allow either he or Pam to drive her, but she refused, telling him she felt perfectly fine and could drive herself.

To hide the inevitable loss of her hair, she began wearing a wig. Penny lived in Mt. Gilead at the time, about an hour's drive from Charlotte. Martha stayed with her during her trips there.

Penny drove her to the hospital in Charlotte for her chemo treatments which involved 4 to 5 daily trips per session. Penny recalled that her mother went through 3 or 4 different treatment plans and had 2 remissions, but she didn't remember any of the plan details or names of the doctors.

Martha tolerated the treatments in good spirits and kept a positive outlook. As the best part of visiting Penny, Martha had the opportunity to spend a lot of time with her 3 grandsons; Wesley, Vincent and Landon, who adored their "Grandy."

The Pac-Man game enjoyed considerable popularity with the boys at the time and as a way of explaining her chemo therapy to them she described it as gobbling up her cancer in the same way the Pac-Man character ate up every-thing in its path.

In spite of the chemo therapy and best efforts of her doctors, the sarcoma kept recurring; first in her lymph nodes, and then in her other organs. While preparing for a new trial at the end of December 1996 through early January of the next year, she had heart and bone scans done at the hospital.

After returning home with Penny from the hospital in the afternoon of Thursday, January 9th, Martha began ex-periencing transitory bouts of breathing distress.

Penny, almost 9 full months pregnant with a baby daughter, had just driven her mother to a store where she bought a Layette for the baby and they were enroute to a hardware store to buy molding Martha wanted to put up in the baby's nursery. Along the way, Martha started having breathing problems.

Penny pulled off the road into a parking lot and they just sat there while Martha tried to catch her breath. After a bit she seemed OK and they continued on to their destination where Martha purchased the molding and some pink paint.

Later in the evening while Penny prepared dinner, Martha had spread newspapers on the kitchen floor and sat on a stool brushing the paint on the 8-foot-long sections of rope-design molding.

As she sat there, her second bout of respiratory dis-tress came on. Seeing her struggling to breathe, Penny sat next to her on the floor and did what she could to help her through the episode, from which she shortly recovered.

Not knowing if, or when, she might have another attack, Penny advised her that she did not need to climb the stairs to the second-floor guest room and she would move her to the master bedroom down stairs.

Martha protested the move as needless, but her daughter ignored her and exchanged their respective overnight necessities between the two rooms.

After her relocation downstairs, Martha lay resting in bed when Ballard came in. He had moved to the area after high school graduation to enroll in a local college.

Having been accepted, he attended orientation at the college that day. As he sat at the foot of Martha's bed telling her of those exciting events, her breathing problems persisted.

Although less severely than earlier, Penny found them worrisome enough to leave the room and call her dad to inform him of the situation. He told her to call the doctor in the morning about what had happened and do whatever he advised.

Martha already had an appointment scheduled with the doctor at 10:00 the next morning so Penny thought it would be OK for her to wait until then to see him. Martha seemed to rest comfortably when they retired for the night.

Very early the next morning, Penny awoke to the sound of her mother's voice calling her. Rushing down to her room, she found her sitting on the edge of the bed very pale and struggling to breathe.

On recognizing her mother's urgent need of medical attention, Penny told her she would call 911 to bring oxygen and an ambulance and maybe they would take her to her doctor's appointment.

Martha replied that she needed to go to the bathroom but could not do so without assistance. Penny complied with her request and after getting her situated in the bathroom, she stepped back into the bedroom to make the 911 call.

With that accomplished, she returned to the bathroom to help Martha back to her bed. But during her short stay there, she had grown worse and as Penny tried helping her back to the bed, Martha told her she needed to sit down.

In response, Penny told her, "Mom, you can't sit on the floor." "No," Martha told her, "I can't make it to the bed, I have to sit on the floor." With that, Penny could only steady her as she went down.

Leaving her where she sat, Penny retrieved a blanket and pillow from her bed. She spread out the blanket for her to lie on and placed the pillow under her head as she sank back onto it.

Within moments, the doorbell rang on arrival of the paramedics. Penny admitted them and ushered them to her mother's side where they wasted no time in getting to work. They immediately began readying a mask through which to supply her the oxygen she desperately needed.

Ballard, who had slept in an upstairs bedroom, came into the room unawares and on seeing him, Penny went out to fill him in. She returned to the bathroom at the moment a paramedic had just placed the oxygen mask on Martha.

Squatting down next to her, and holding her hand, Penny asked if that was better. "Much better," Martha replied.

Those were the last words Penny would ever hear her mother say, because within the next few minutes she went into cardiac arrest. The paramedics gave her CPR and managed to resuscitate her, after which they began preparing to load her in the ambulance.

Penny, still in her pajamas, hurried into another room and dressed as directed by one of the paramedics who told her she needed to do that if she planned to follow the ambulance to the hospital with her mother.

She and Ballard followed in his car. On arriving at the hospital, they learned Martha had gone into cardiac arrest a second time in the ambulance and in spite of their best efforts, the paramedics failed to get her heart started again. Her life ended on Friday morning, January 10th, 1997.

Penny called her dad to give him the sad news. In the meantime, Penny's former husband, whom she was in the process of divorcing, arranged for his company plane to fly to DeFuniak Springs and pick Jimmy up and bring him to Mt. Gilead.

Jimmy went to the airport to await the fast twin engine plane. On its arrival he boarded and within an hour or so found himself at the hospital in record time.

In conversations with Penny before she died, Martha told her she did not want Jimmy involved with what was happening to her, but refused to explain why. She made

Penny promise that in the event of her death, not to allow Jimmy to see her without her wig.

When Jimmy arrived at the hospital, Penny dutifully informed him of her mother's wishes, which he ignored and went immediately to the side of his wife of almost 40 years lying deceased in a hospital bed.

She fought the cancer for more than 3 years, but in the end, it did not directly cause her death. Her doctors surmised instead, that she died of anaphylactic shock from an allergic reaction to the dyes in the scans at the hospital.

Also, Dr. Robert Sheppard thought she might have suffered a pulmonary embolism from a clot that formed in her pelvic area and migrated to her lungs.

Their mother's death devastated Penny and Ballard. On the day she died, Penny had been pregnant with her own daughter, India, just short of 9 full months. She gave birth to her on January 31st, 21 days too late for Martha to meet her first baby granddaughter.

The strained relationship between her parents baffled Penny. She could get no explanation from either of them as to its reason. When she and her siblings were growing up, their parents never aired their differences in front of their children, but did it privately behind closed doors.

That situation had changed however, by the time Martha underwent her treatments in North Carolina. For a number of years prior to her cancer diagnosis, she grew increasingly irritable toward Jimmy and the children remaining at home after Penny moved away and started her own family.

Because of the considerable distance between her home and that of her parents, she remained largely unaware of the abject rancor dominating the estrangement that had grown between them over the last 10 or 12 years of her mother's life.

She did not know her mother had abandoned all discretion in venting her anger at Jimmy and he at her. Jimmy recalled that their relationship had grown so antagonistic that their children still at home asked him why they didn't just get a divorce.

Ballard didn't recall seeing that behavior between his parents very often, but remembered many shouting matches between himself and his mother. He admitted in retrospect though, that as a rebellious teenager, he could not hold himself blameless.

Perhaps the most shocking revelation about her mother came from Pam. She recalled that as a toddler she progressed too slowly in her potty training to suit her mother. Becoming angry at her for that, Martha grabbed her by the hair and dunked her head in the toilet. After pulling her out, she shook her severely and shoved her backwards.

Pam never told anyone about it until she grew up because she thought no one would believe her. Later in life, she told her uncle, Martha's brother, about it and he told her that their mother had done the same thing to them as children.

The treatment sounds reminiscent of what some people believe about rubbing a puppy's nose in the spot where he wet the carpet to break him from doing it.

Pam never forgot the incident and when she graduated from college, she loaded all she owned in her pickup and moved to California.

Penny apparently never saw the side of her mom that her dad and Pam did, probably because of the close relationship she had with her mother.

She seems also to have been unaware that her parents had considered divorcing. But Martha's expressed views on the subject led Jimmy to believe that termination of the marriage would leave him without access to or involvement in the lives of his children.

That possibility, more than any demands on his financial or other assets she might make, he found totally unacceptable.

She had her own reasons unfavorable to divorce, not the least of which was the social life she so highly valued. As a doctor's wife, she enjoyed a certain level of prestige which might be diminished if they divorced. But she had other reasons as well.

She understood as Jimmy did that many of the positive relationship aspects woven into their family as a unit might be damaged or lost in a divorce, especially in regard to the children. That, she found unacceptable, making her more amenable to a solution other than ending the marriage.

On coming to the realization that divorce might lead to consequences neither of them wanted, they settled on living apart as a better solution. That led to the purchase of the town house in Niceville and Martha and Ballard moving there from the farm.

But even then, Jimmy often stayed with them in Niceville sometimes for weeks at the time depending on his work schedule and they frequently came to the farm and spent time there.

When Martha came down with cancer, she seemed determined to keep Jimmy at arm's length during her therapy, to which Jimmy seemed to acquiesce. Penny put the blame on him, thinking Martha a victim of his insensitivity without realizing her mother's culpability in the standoff.

Ballard didn't see his mother as the type of person who would think of herself as a victim under any circumstances. She was too strong for that, he believed. He described his parents as juggernauts of strength and independence, neither of which looked to the other for much of anything.

Yet, Penny felt Jimmy had wronged her mother by his lack of support when she needed it and remained bitter toward him long after her mother passed. How she felt about her father however, may have been only one item on her list of grievances.

In addition to dealing with her mother's illness and death, her husband had recently decided he wanted out of their marriage and deserted her with 3 young sons and pregnant with a baby daughter.

That left her as a single mother on whose shoulders fell the burden of providing for her children's needs and wants. She may have even felt wronged as she thought her mother had been.

With perceived wrongs nearing the unbearable, she felt the need to separate herself from the place she knew she could never again look back upon without pain.

That led her to pack up her belongings and move with her children to an Indian reservation on Washington State's Olympic Peninsula bordering the Pacific Ocean, where she hoped to make a new start.

The name of the reservation is Quinault, for the Native Americans of that name who are its owners and occupants. Penny and a business partner established the Quinault Guide Service in a little place called Amanda Park on the shores of Lake Quinault, from which the river of the same name flows a few miles to the southwest into the Pacific Ocean.

Aberdeen, the nearest town of any size to Amanda Park, is 109 miles southwest of Seattle and 77 miles north of Astoria, in giving perspective to its general location.

The house Penny occupied on moving there in 1997 about the time India turned a year old, belongs to the business partnership into which she entered at the time.

But under treaty law, she was not allowed to personally own it. She owns 50% of the business however, which is allowable under applicable law.

While living there, her children attended the K-12 Amanda Park School with class sizes averaging 5-8 students each. The proximity of Penny's work in relation to the school put her close enough to quickly reach it in case of an emergency, thereby minimizing her time away from the business.

The business began as a fishing and hunting guide service on tribal lands and waters, as well as the Pacific Ocean. The service took 2 different forms. One involved the use of small river boats which took customers out in search of several species of salmon, steelhead and trout.

The other required larger oceangoing vessels for Pacific excursions in quest of crab, halibut, black cod and tuna. The business has done well and Penny still holds an ownership interest in it.

The area is at the foot of the Olympic Mountains and abounds in places to hike and camp, many of which became familiar to Penny. After moving there from North Carolina, she phoned her dad to let him know where she had gone even though she still harbored ill feelings toward him.

Out of concern for her, he showed up unannounced for a visit sometime around 1998. Still very angry with him because, as she put it, he, "checked out," on her mom, she decided to take him on a hike over a "brutal trail," she knew about in an attempt to punish him.

Finishing the hike around noon and hoping he had gotten the message; she took him to a local mercantile store and deli for lunch.

Over soup and sandwiches, she unloaded on him, capping off their spirited jaunt with the words she thought justified it. She pointed out his seeming indifference to her mother's suffering and all the hurts for which she held him responsible.

At the end of the conversation, however, her view of him had changed from how she perceived him when it began. That left her more at peace with the man she saw for the first time that day as a person and not just her dad.

In the years since, the two of them have talked through the "hurts and pains, and have come out on the other side with many memories of joy and peace," as Penny put it.

"We also came to an understanding that we both were devastated by my mother's death, and I have tried to acknowledge that we were both dealing with her illness and death in our own ways. He's my dad, and I have a great respect for him," she concluded.

When Martha died, Ballard, at age 19, had just entered college. Jimmy thought it important that he realize his life would never again be the same as when his mother lived. After her memorial service in Ft. Walton, Jimmy sat down with him to make that clear.

He spoke to him about how his mother had waited on him, catered to him and otherwise spoiled him. She had done that, Jimmy told him, because she loved him so much that she could deny him nothing,

Ballard just sat there looking at his father. Jimmy went on, telling him he may have been spoiled as a child, but acting that way as an adult would not be in his best interest. He told him it would be just the two of them the rest of the way and he wanted to let him know their relationship would not be the same as it had been between he and his mother.

"You know me well enough by now not to expect me to tolerate that, so let's just put that aside and get rid of it and act like adults," Jimmy concluded, having gotten what he had to say off his chest.

"Dad," Ballard responded, "you have always treated me well and I love you. You were right about everything I ever talked to you about. You have made few mistakes in your life and whatever you say is the way it is going to be."

Ballard recalled the conversation, but his spirits were so low on the loss of the most important person in his life at the time that he barely felt like replying at all to his dad.

When he responded the way he did though, it became Jimmy's turn to sit staring. If he had expected a fiery Lola response, the one his son gave him sounded more like the gentle Arthur instead. He could not have been more pleased.

With regard to Lola, Jimmy harbored no shame that he carried a heavy dose of her personality in his genetic heritage and there were times when it showed, especially if a government man or politician came to the farm.

He recalled the time, for instance, when a man identifying himself as the Agricultural agent drove up in the yard. He told Jimmy he needed to measure the peanut acreage. Jimmy told him no, he would do no measuring of anything. The agent told him he had the legal right to measure the acreage of peanuts he intended to sell.

Jimmy responded that he only grew a couple acres of peanuts for the kids to boil, to sell to super markets and at a road side stand.

As long as he did not sell them to a government support buyer at government support prices, he had no obligation to allow the government to measure his acreage and the agent had worn out his welcome and should leave.

He found his mother's tendencies in himself the most irrepressible when it came to politicians. He believed that no politician except George Washington ever cared about individual American interests.

All politicians after him looked out for themselves, including John Adams and his son, John Quincy, both of whom followed Washington in the presidency.

Any time a politician drove into Jimmy's yard and stepped from his car with his hand stuck out, he met the scorn of Lola Clyde replete with her choice of words rather than the hospitality and grace of Arthur, thus incentivizing a speedy departure.

IV

≈BRUCE CREEK FARM≈

A Menagerie, Battling John Deer, Diamond T,
The Cattle Business Hobby, The IRS, An Eleven
Thousand Dollar Tractor Restoration, A Cabin in
Oregon and A Second Marriage.

Government agents and politicians may have found
the farm short on hospitality, but not so the Sheppard children. Living there to them seemed just one big adventure.
They had acres and acres of beautiful scenery in which to
roam and explore.

Bruce Creek, as it zigzagged its way across the farm,
beckoned them to refreshing swims in its cool waters when
stifling summer heat wore on them. The farm gave them
more than enough space for all the pets their hearts desired
and could care for.

They had a menagerie of animals; horses, chickens,
ducks, geese, rabbits, peacocks, turkeys, deer, foxes and others. They had one old wild turkey hatched from an egg they
stole out of a nest in the woods.

Jimmy bought them an incubator to hatch the egg which they succeeded in doing. The hatchling grew up to be a 30-pound gobbler who loved nothing better than to torment the kids.

He would puff himself up into his finest feathered glory with his tail fanned out as in a Thanksgiving print, making himself appear deceptively large. As a bluff, he would strut at the children with fluttering wings; trying to put a scare into them.

They finally came to recognize his boisterous displays as nothing more than harmless antics, meant to intimidate them if he could.

Not only did Jimmy's children love animals, but he brought his own affection for them as a boy to his adulthood. That became evident when someone brought two red fox cubs they had dug out of a den to the farm and offered to sell them to Jimmy.

He told the man he usually avoided buying wild animals because he wanted to discourage people from digging up more of them.

But he bought them anyway for 10 dollars figuring they had a better chance of surviving with him than if left with the guy wanting to sell them. This happened during one extremely cold winter when temperatures dropped well below freezing at night.

He had made the cubs a bed in a cardboard box but gave them too little bedding to stay warm. When they got cold and began crying in the middle of the night, he brought them to his bed and put them under the cover between himself and Martha.

Their squirming about wakened Martha and she asked Jimmy what he had put in their bed. The fox cubs, he told her. He put them there to stay warm, because they cried and whined in the cold and he didn't know what else to do with them.

He and the children kept them well fed and nurtured and by spring they had grown quite a bit. So that they could stay outside and get the exercise they needed, Jimmy built them an enclosed trace, like a dog run, about a hundred feet long, of chicken wire.

It gave them a place where not only could they get the exercise they needed but also become familiar with the natural surroundings they would soon be released into.

In the evenings when he came home from work, Jimmy turned them out. They ran around in the yard and played just as puppies would. At dark he put them back because every night fox hunters released their hounds to run wild foxes near the farm. With the hounds about, the trace kept the pet foxes safe when very young.

In an attempt to stop fox hunters from letting their dogs run on his property, Jimmy posted it in the manner prescribed by Florida law to make it legally binding against anyone entering it without one or the other of his verbal or written permission.

Early on when he planned on going into farming and stock raising, he had fenced in the entire farm which required 40 rolls of wire and 4 thousand fence posts. The postings against trespassing came later, and Jimmy recruited Penny, then in high school, to put them up on fence posts along the road. She recalled that as she went along stapling them to the posts, she began hearing gunshots.

As she stood watching, a pickup drove slowly along the road with several young men brandishing guns in the back shooting down the signs she had just put up. Not content with vandalizing the signs, many hunters blatantly ignored them and turned their dogs loose on the property anyway.

Because of that, leaving the pet foxes out overnight put them at risk from the hounds, but Jimmy thought it best they learn to fend for themselves so when they eventually returned to the wild, they would at least have a chance to survive.

As they grew older, he gave them more liberty and eventually they had the run of the farm. When the family came home in the evenings from work and school, the foxes followed them into the house and the kids played with them as if they were dogs.

Over time, they adapted to life on their own and spent less time with the family. Occasionally they could be seen at the far end of the horse pasture frolicking and jumping over each other in a fox's version of leap frog. The point finally came, however when they disappeared completely from the farm and were not seen anymore.

Another orphan arrived on Jimmy's door step, in a manner of speaking, when a wild life officer dropped a fawn off at the farm. The officer, after arresting the man who illegally shot its mother, found it lying under a bush. Knowing it would not survive on its own, he brought it to the farm hoping the Sheppards would take it in and care for it.

Telling Jimmy he knew him to be a sucker for lost causes, he had another one for him, as the fawn, newly born, probably could not be saved without its mother. A tiny little thing no bigger than a house cat, white spots serving as protective camouflage in the wild covered its back.

Nothing is more adorable than an infant white tail deer and the whole family fell in love with it. The girls made it a bed in a cardboard box. They placed it between their beds so they could feed it when it got hungry at night.

Jimmy looked up the formula for reindeer milk in his medical journal and came up with his own substitute for it. Diluting canned "Pet Milk," with water and adding a little sugar, he tinkered with the formula until the fawn seemed to like it. The girls fed it to him from a bottle until he got old enough to eat other foods.

He grew rapidly and remained a house pet until no longer practical to keep him inside. Like the foxes had been, he became a playmate to the children. That included Ballard whose birth preceded the fawn's by probably no more than a year and a half.

Evidence of that came from a local newspaper photo of he and his mother bottle feeding the less than half grown fawn still wearing its white spots. The photo caption gave Ballard's age as 2 at the time and identified the fawn as Bambi.

When they took the deer out of the house, they put him in a horse stall in the big barn and kept him there for a while. Later on, Jimmy built a fenced enclosure of about 3 acres in size as a pen for him to stay in. Even though the fence stood as high as 6 or 8 feet, the deer when full-grown, easily sprang over it.

When he reached adulthood, the children changed his named from Bambi to John Deer because with his antlers he resembled the logo on their dad's favorite tractor. It sounded the same but with a slightly different spelling.

An incident involving John Deer brought Jimmy more grief with hunting dogs running on his property. The family returned home from church one Sunday to find hounds chasing the buck around in his enclosure. When he saw the family arrive at the house, he bounded over the fence and raced toward them for protection from the dogs.

The fence slowed the dogs momentarily, but they got passed it and resumed the chase. When the family opened the door to go into the house, the buck darted inside. His hooves immediately skidded on the vinyl floor, causing him to fall and go sliding on his flank. Before coming to a stop, he knocked over every chair and piece of furniture in his path.

The chasing dogs had so exhausted him that he could hardly get up. Frothing profusely at the mouth, he breathed heavily as he struggled unsteadily to his feet.

Jimmy thought that for him to be so thoroughly ex-hausted, the dogs apparently had chased him for quite a while. That thought angering him, Jimmy grabbed his shotgun and began shooting every hound in sight as he stepped out the door. He regretted it afterwards because he realized that instead of the dogs, he should have blamed the men who owned them.

The dogs didn't know any better, but the men did. As an animal lover himself, it sickened him to think he had allowed his temper to make him do something that under normal circumstances he would have found abhorrent.

The owners of the dogs Jimmy shot went to county judge Clyde Wells wanting to file a complaint against him for killing their dogs. But when the judge learned that Jimmy had fenced and posted his property in accordance with the law, he refused to accept the complaint and came down hard on the dog owners instead.

He told them Jimmy had the law fully on his side. Instead of them filing a complaint against him, he should be filing one against them for letting their dogs loose on property clearly and legally posted against trespassing. Under the circumstances, Jimmy had every right to take the action he did to protect his property against the damage the dogs could have done if he had not stopped them.

Having survived the dogs on that occasion, and under Jimmy's care and protection, John Deer lived to the ripe old age of 16. A wild life officer told Jimmy a buck in the wild who managed to survived hunters lived an average life span of about half that number of years.

Other than for one notable exception, the buck remained as docile as a lamb his entire life although he possessed the strength and instincts to be a dangerous animal.

Just how dangerous, Jimmy learned one spring when he went missing from his pen. Going in search of him, Jimmy found where he had gone through the fence at a floating gate he had built across the creek running through the pen.

During recent rains, rising waters in the creek had caused the gate to open. But when the water receded the gate, blocked by debris deposited by the high water, failed to close, allowing the deer to get out.

Jimmy found him a short distance up the creek with several does which ran when he approached. Ever since he was a fawn, John Deer had loved cookies and Jimmy always carried several in his shirt pocket to give him.

Jimmy expected him to come and eat the cookie he held out to him as he normally would, but that time he just stood looking at him.

Jimmy walked over and gave him the cookie, which he ate. Then, to his surprise, the buck charged and knocked him to the ground. Getting up, Jimmy found his behavior baffling because in the past the deer would "follow him to the ends of the earth for a cookie."

He held another cookie out to the deer and again, the buck lowered his antlers and charged, knocking Jimmy backwards into the creek behind him.

Making matters worse, as Jimmy floundered in the waist deep water, the deer plunged into the creek on top of him. Putting out his forearms in defense of the buck's pummeling antlers against his chest and face, he succeeded in warding off any serious injuries to himself.

In an effort to get the 200-pound animal off him, he grabbed his antlers and shoved him away so he could get his head above water. But the deer did not wait for him to get to his feet before hitting him again. At that point, Jimmy began thinking himself in serious trouble because the deer apparently held murderous intentions toward him.

Pushing the animal off again, Jimmy reached up and grabbed a nearby sapling growing from the bank to pull himself out of the water. No sooner had he clambered out onto the bank than the buck launched another assault, slamming him to the ground yet again.

It became obvious to Jimmy the deer had no intention of ending the attack on his own. He looked around for a limb or piece of wood of some kind to use as a weapon, but saw nothing within reach.

When the deer came at him again, Jimmy knew his best chance would be to grab him by his antlers and just hold on. When he did that, the deer in trying to shake him loose, tossed his head back, lifted Jimmy's feet off the ground and swung him about as if he weighed nothing.

Their struggles took them near a pine tree about 6 inches in diameter. Reaching out and hooking his arm around the tree, Jimmy pulled the Deer's neck up against it and tried his best to wrap it around the trunk.

To apply greater pressure, he placed his knee against his neck and held it there until the deer began wheezing for breath. He continued choking him until he passed out and fell to the ground.

Not wanting to hang around and give the deer another shot at him, Jimmy climbed over the fence and once on the other side, waited to make sure he revived. When he saw him begin to move, he went on to the house and attended to his injuries.

Undressing and getting into the shower, he counted 5 holes in his body. He had one in his forehead, 2 or 3 in his chest and abdomen, and one in his side. All of them being superficial, as miraculous as that may have seemed, he needed no medication other than a liberal application of merthiolate. Thanks to his reasonably good physical condition, he had absorbed the buck's punishment without more serious injuries.

After giving himself first aid, he got his shotgun and headed back to the buck's pen. If the deer caused any more trouble, Jimmy vowed to make him pay for it the next time rather than himself. He usually fed the buck about that time of the day.

When he arrived at the pen the deer had gone back inside the fence and awaited his daily feeding as if nothing had happened. Jimmy reached through the fence and scratched the animal's head as he had done numerous times before and he showed no hint of his earlier hostility.

The buck attacked him, Jimmy concluded, due to it being the rutting season when his instincts drove him to breed. When Jimmy walked up on him with his does, the buck saw him as another buck challenging him for his females, to which he responded as instinctively compelled. Having been raised from a fawn by Jimmy and his family, the buck probably drew no distinction between humans and deer.

A game warden later told Jimmy, after hearing of the deer attacking him, that supposedly tame male deer had killed many people. They should be considered dangerous due to the risk of provoking them out of ignorance as Jimmy had done.

Jimmy found another animal that represented an even deadlier threat if provoked in one of his open tractor sheds. He parked his unrestored tractors under those sheds and used them for replacement parts for the tractors he re-stored.

One day when removing a part from one of the trac-tors, he happened to glance down at the ground where he stood. To his horror a huge diamond back rattle snake lay coiled only inches from his foot.

His hair standing up on the back of his neck, he very, very slowly and carefully backed out of the shed. At no time did the snake raise its head, sound its rattles, or show any inclination to strike.

Jimmy surmised it did not because it had inhabited the shed for a time before he discovered it. During that pe-riod, it grew accustomed to his comings and goings and viewed him as unthreatening.

Jimmy thought that probably explained why it re-mained unprovoked at his close proximity to it when found out. The snake took up residence in the shed because it found a food source in the many wharf rats and squirrels that built their nests in the tractor battery and tool boxes.

The rodents chewed holes in tractor seats and ate the insulation from electrical wires, reducing the value of the tractors as a source of replacement parts, and generally left a mess in the shed.

Jimmy decided eating the rodents made the snake more beneficial to him than killing it, so he let it alone and even gave it a name. He called it "Diamond T," in memory of the neighbor's truck he drove as a farm boy.

In future visits to the shed however, he thoroughly scrutinized his intended path into it to for any sign of the snake before entering and he warned other family members to avoid the shed at all costs.

The snake remained in the shed for a couple of years but eventually died, apparently of old age. Jimmy later came across its bones in the pasture near the shed and on applying his measuring tape, found it to be over 7 feet long with 20 rattles and a button.

Just thinking of what might have happened if he had stepped on the snake the day he discovered it long remained almost too frightening to contemplate in Jimmy's mind.

Many animals of the wild variety found a haven in Bruce Creek swamp, a portion of which spread over several acres of the farm. One, a 12-foot alligator, brought an end to the children swimming in the creek upon its discovery.

The gradual disappearance of mallard ducks released on the creek by a wildlife officer mystified the family. They finally figured out an alligator preyed on the ducks when his large foot prints and tail dragging marks showed up on the sandy banks of the creek.

Sharing the creek with the alligator were several beavers and otters, whom Jimmy often watched play in the water from his back deck overlooking the stream. The agile animals had no fear of the alligator because they easily out swam and out maneuvered him

The sights, sounds and smells of domestic animals and fowls on the farm sometimes became an irresistible temptation to other hungry predators lurking at the edge of the swamp. Bobcats proved the most frequent offenders.

Jimmy found it necessary to trap several of them which he transported far enough away from the farm to not find their way back and set them free.

One ferocious old bobcat he caught almost out did Diamond T in raising Jimmy's hackles. As he approached the trap, the bobcat inside let out a vicious, blood curdling snarl and angrily raked the side of the wire cage with his claws.

Looking into the animal's fiery eyes sent chills up Jimmy's back. He felt comforted that the good, strong steel wire of the trap stood between himself and its decidedly unhappy occupant. He loaded the trap onto his pickup and transported to the release site.

There he removed it from the truck and set it on the ground. In an abundance of caution, he tied a long string to the door of the trap and moved to a point about 10 feet behind it from where he pulled the string to open the door and free the animal.

The bobcat watched Jimmy so intently that it took him few seconds to look around and see the open exit. But instead of bolting through it, he casually walked out. He stopped momentarily and looked back at Jimmy as if expecting something else preventing him from going free to happen, and when it did not, he continued unhurriedly on his way and disappeared into the brush.

In a couple of instances, instead of bobcats, their scarcer cousins showed up at the farm. Rather than keeping the many pet rabbits the children raised penned up, they released them to run free on the grounds.

One day Polly heard a rabbit squealing and going to investigate, she came face-to-face with a Florida panther making a meal of the hapless bunny. To her good fortune, the panther preferred eating rabbits that day and not young girls.

On another occasion, Jimmy sighted a panther crossing the road near Bruce Creek bridge. Driving home in his car, he approached within 50 feet of it before it ran into the woods on his property. He got close enough to positively identify it as a panther.

When Jimmy moved to the farm, he had in mind other animals he wanted to raise. He built the big barn in anticipation of using it to house equipment and supplies needed in the cattle business he planned to start as a sideline to his medical practice.

He began prepping his land for planting corn and grass so that when he bought his cattle, he would have feed for them. In 1978 he took the first step in building his herd with the purchase of a dozen pure-bred Charolais cattle. Between that year and 1990, his herd grew to 27 head.

That year the IRS showed up and audited him. He had been claiming his farm expenses as a write-off against his medical practice income. The IRS determined that his farming operations met the definition of a hobby and as such, their rules did not allow him to claim those expenses as deductions against his tax liability.

They presented him with a claim of a million dollars in back taxes and interest they said he owed. He told them if they tried to pursue collecting that amount, he would demand a trial by jury of 12 men from among his farmer-neighbors who were doing the same thing he was doing and see if the IRS could win the case.

The IRS, aware that he possessed the resources to mount a strong defense against them, apparently decided not to risk losing to him in a court battle and reduced the amount he owed dramatically. They ended up settling with him for less than 4 hundred dollars

That close encounter with the IRS made Jimmy rethink the direction in which he headed with farming and led to a change in his interests. His medical practice kept him busy, but he needed something to do in his off time. That objective had motivated him to try the cattle business as a side line and when it failed to work out, he looked for something else.

He did not realize it at the time, but he had begun dabbling in what would become his new interest not long after moving to the farm. A guy he knew in Ft. Walton had an old John Deere tractor sitting behind his house rusting away. He offered to sell it to Jimmy but on going to see it, he found a piece of junk and told the guy no thanks.

Afterwards, the man came down to Jimmy's office and told him he would make him a deal on the tractor. If Jimmy would haul it off, the man said, he could have it for nothing. Thinking it might be worth that, Jimmy took his trailer down and brought it back to the farm.

In looking at the tractor, it appeared complete to Jimmy with all its parts intact. Everything just seemed rusty and he thought he could restore it. Deciding to give it a try, he took it apart, cleaned everything of rust as best he could, and began trying to put it back together.

The rust damage on many parts however, rendered them unserviceable. That required him to replace them with new parts, which he had to buy at retail prices.

In view of what the parts cost him, Jimmy thought it wise to make sure of their proper installation because if he went to the trouble and expense of restoring it, he wanted a fully functioning tractor when done with it.

Uncertain at that point of his mechanical knowledge to properly restore the tractor, he told the dealer he needed somebody to help him put it back together and asked if he knew anybody who might be able to do that.

The dealer told him their 70-year-old service manager had recently retired. After many years of working on 2-cylinder John Deere tractors he had become good at it and might be interested in helping, the dealer said.

The man agreed to help and 11 thousand dollars later at dealer retail parts prices and dealer hourly labor rates, Jimmy had his fully restored, functioning tractor.

He realized he could have done better by finding a tractor in fairly good shape that still ran. He could have bought and restored it for a couple of thousand dollars and come out many thousands ahead. That taught him a lesson on how not to restore tractors.

In spite of what it cost him to restore the tractor, he enjoyed doing it and began gravitating in that direction. Deciding to continue with it after becoming disenchanted with cattle, he started looking for more tractors to restore.

He became acquainted with Zane Sunday of Glendale, once the superintendent of the Walton County district school system.

Zane had a model 40 John Deere he used on his farm. It developed problems which his mechanic brother thought a new 6-hundred-dollar crankshaft would fix. But Zane refused to pay that for a part he thought would cost more than the worth of the tractor. Deciding he would come out better to get rid of it, he sold it to Jimmy for half the cost of a new crankshaft.

Shortly thereafter, Jimmy acquired a second tractor of the same model with a transmission that had been damaged when the mower behind it hit a stump.

Its engine still mechanically sound, Jimmy cleaned it and put it in the Zane Sunday tractor, ending up with a completely restored machine in perfect operating condition.

As he gained experience in locating restorable tractors, he found the best ones came from places where low humidity and sparse rain fall caused less rusting in those machines sitting out in the weather, where old tractors more often than not ultimately ended up. Those places tended to be in the Midwest and western regions of the country.

The U. S. west coast is such a place and sometime around 1998 Jimmy spent some time visiting Penny on the Indian reservation to where she had moved after her divorce. On the same trip he visited an old friend holding an auction of old Caterpillars and John Deeres in Spokane, Washington, about 170 miles north of Wala Wala, in the northeast corner of the state.

After the auction, he had a couple of days to kill before his flight back home. He came across a western newspaper on farming and ranching in Oregon in which he found an ad for 171 acres of recreational property for sale in the Blue Mountains near Pendleton.

He had never been to those places before and decided to drive down in his rental car and check them out. On arrival at the Pendleton address listed in the ad, he walked into the real estate office and asked to speak to Robin, whom the ad identified as the person to see.

The individual he addressed directed him to an office down the hall. When he knocked on the door a voice behind it told him to come in. He entered and announced to the man he assumed to be Robin that he had seen the ad for 171 acres for sale in the Blue Mountains and wanted to know if it remained available.

On hearing Jimmy's southern accent, the man responding to the name, Robin, leaned forward and asked "where are you from?" ignoring the query about the land.

Jimmy replied; "Robin, the way you said that makes me know you know I am not from here." "That's true," Robin said. "I am from Florida and we have snowbirds there that come from the northeast and I am a sunbird from Florida here to buy a piece of land and you guys need some visitors from the south. They are scarce out here," Jimmy told him.

Robin laughed, saying "That's good, I like that. You are the first southerner to ever walk into this office." Finally getting around to Jimmy's question about the land, Robin told him the ad ran out 3 months earlier and not relisted, but he thought the property might still be for sale.

If he would like to see the property, they could drive up to it and he could make the owner an offer, he told Jimmy.

Jimmy responded in the affirmative and after an hour's drive into the mountains, they came to a gate across a logging road. Nodding at the gate, Robin told Jimmy to go through it and follow the trail a quarter of a mile to an open meadow. Beyond that, he would come to the Wala Wala River canyon, located near the eastern end of the property.

Following the directions given him, Jimmy soon found himself on the property, which greeted him with possibly the most beautiful scenery he had ever laid eyes on.

The immense canyon it overlooked with the river coursing through it far below offered a breath-taking view that "just kind of stole my heart," as he put it. Not only did he find the property beautiful, but it seemed to stretch "way out at the ends of the earth," another reason he liked it.

He made his way back to Robin's vehicle and asked him the owner's listed price. "He wanted 120 thousand for it," Robin replied, "but before his ad expired, he told us he would take less." Jimmy suggested they offer 90 thousand for it. To his surprise, the owner accepted and Jimmy happily bought it.

He purchased the property with the aim of building a vacation cabin on it. But before doing any building, he had to apply to the state of Oregon for a permit to put up a structure in the mountains. In turn, he had to have the state permit in hand before he could apply for a building permit on the property in its home county of Umatilla.

To get things rolling as soon as possible, he applied to the state of Oregon for a permit. They responded with a request for his last 3 years of income tax returns to "prove I would not be a ward of the state."

The sarcasm came from Jimmy because he thought the bureaucrats wanting his tax returns indicated they did not think a doctor qualified to buy a piece of land because he might be a freeloader. But he complied and sent them copies of his returns as requested.

It took the state a year to approve the permit. When it came, Jimmy took it to the Umatilla County seat to apply for their permit. First, they told him, he needed to give them a set of plans drawn by a draftsman. Anticipating that, he brought the plans with him and on handing them over got his permit.

With the permit hurdles finally cleared he started work on the cabin. He wanted it to be the most unique of its kind in Oregon, and nothing could be more unique to that state than a cabin built of antique cypress lumber from the Florida panhandle.

He went home and rented a 26-foot Penske moving truck; the biggest they had, loaded it with the cypress lumber he had stored in his big barn since the mid 1970s, and headed back to Oregon with it.

When he got there, he hired a one-man contractor with a helper to do most of the building. He worked on it some of the time himself, but due to the demands of his practice back home, he could not stay there during the entire time required to finish it.

He finished the cabin in 2001. A year earlier, he met Elizabeth Barton, the woman who would become his second wife. He met her in Fresno, California while on a trip to a tractor show in nearby Tulare.

Born and raised in Ft. Walton Beach, Florida, Liz held almost 3 college degrees in the field of speech pathology; a bachelors, a masters and lacked only 12 hours for her PHD.

Previously, she had worked for the Okaloosa County school system, but had lost her job there and gone to Fresno where she secured a position as school principal. She had been married but divorced in her early thirties.

Her two children from the marriage were grown. She later had 3 grandchildren, 2 of whom were her daughter's and 1 who belonged to her son. She lost her mother to

Alzheimer's and not long afterwards, her younger brother fell victim to the disease.

Jimmy learned about her from her best friend who also worked for the Okaloosa County school system. Jimmy knew the friend as a patient and acquaintance from his Ft. Walton practice.

When he casually mentioned his planned Tulare trip to her, she told him about Liz and urged him to meet her while out there. Liz felt so homesick for Ft. Walton, she told him, that she received several calls a week from her.

She gave Jimmy Liz' phone number so he could call and introduce himself. Before leaving on the trip, he phoned with his introduction, which her school board friend, of course, had notified her in advance to expect.

Jimmy explained the reason for his call, which he suspected she already knew, also from their mutual Ft. Walton friend. She confirmed his suspicion when she said she knew who he was. He advised that when he landed in Fresno, he would ring her again to arrange a meeting and make further plans.

When he arrived in Fresno, he first phoned his friends Robby and Doris Soults in Tulare whom he had met some years earlier. They shared his interest in antique tractors and on those occasions when he visited the area, he usually got together with them at a local restaurant. They especially liked a very nice Fresno eatery called "Sweet Tomatoes," and loved dining there.

He told them of his plans to meet Liz at Sweet Tomatoes and invited them to drive up to the restaurant and join them for what he hoped would be a pleasant evening out. They liked the idea and told him they would leave right away.

After hanging up with them he dialed Liz to inform her of the plans. She knew the restaurant; she told him and would meet him there after work around 5 p. m. He needed to pick up a rental car, and by the time he did that and drove to the restaurant he should get there a little before 5, he advised.

That being satisfactory to her, they said their good byes and hung up. As soon as Jimmy finished the rental car paper work, he headed for the restaurant.

Arriving at the restaurant a few minutes ahead of his appointed time with Liz, Jimmy seated himself on a bench outside the entrance. Shortly he saw Robby and Doris pull into the parking lot.

Even though they waved to him, they did not immediately exit their vehicle and walk over to where he sat. Momentarily another car drove up and parked.

The woman driving it got out and walked toward the entrance. Easily standing over 6 foot tall and weighing probably in excess of 3 hundred pounds, Jimmy's heart sank at the sight of her.

Fearing her to be Liz, but desperately hoping her not to be, he turned his gaze groundward and put his hand over his face to avoid eye contact with her. He breathed a happy sigh of relief when she walked past him and entered the restaurant.

Glancing over at Robby and Doris' truck, he noticed it seemed to be rocking. Looking closer he recognized Robby as the culprit. Easily tipping the scales at 4 hundred pounds, he laughed so hard at Jimmy's reaction to the sight of the large woman that he set the truck to rocking in unison with his hilarity.

Later in the restaurant when Robby kidded him about the incident, Jimmy retaliated with a reference to Robby in the derogatory term meaning someone born out of wedlock.

When the next car drove up and parked, a very attractive woman got out. Even if she had not been Liz, the sensation her appearance elicited in Jimmy wafted over him as a blast of fresh spring air bearing the aroma of sweet honey suckles, in comparison to how the woman arriving before her made him feel.

But Liz she proved to be and he could not have been happier to see her. Martha had been gone over 4 years by then, and if a relationship developed with the lovely woman walking his way that evening, she could expect no resistance from him.

The relationship blossomed and after enjoying each other's company for about a year, according to Jimmy, Liz initiated its next phase when she asked him if there was a chance he would ever consider marrying her.

They had a great deal in common; both were well educated, had good jobs, were financially secure, compatible personality wise and strong affections had grown between them.

He told her he would marry her, but suggested they enter into a prenuptial agreement to protect the assets they each brought into the marriage, to which she agreed. They had an attorney prepare the document, they both signed it and the attorney recorded it at the court house.

These events took place about the time Jimmy finished the cabin in Oregon. In 2002, they decided to fly out there, get married and spend their honeymoon in the cabin.

On arriving in Pendleton, they went to the county judge's office and asked him to marry them. Afterwards, they drove up to the cabin and Liz, on seeing it the first time, was blown away.

She thought it the most beautiful place she had ever seen. The massive canyon dominated the view from the cabin window. It seemed to go on forever, instantly sweeping the eye 50 miles distant and on to "the ends of the earth," as Jimmy liked to describe it. No houses, roads, or anything man-made spoiled the view.

Anytime day or night, all manner of wildlife roamed outside the house. Deer, elk, bobcats, wild turkeys, grouse and pheasants to name a few. The occupants of the cabin felt themselves right there in the midst of the animals, who unaware of their observers, behaved naturally.

On one occasion when driving back to the cabin from town, they spotted a grey wolf lying on a boulder above the road. One old 500-pound moss-back black bear just came up in the yard and grunted while Jimmy, who happened to be in the barn, watched him from the window.

Prior to the bear's arrival, the peculiar behavior of a doe in the yard outside the barn had aroused Jimmy's curiosity. She seemed frozen in place as she peered intently at something beyond Jimmy's view. As he watched, she suddenly bolted and disappeared from sight. When the bear appeared, Jimmy realized why the doe had departed so hurriedly.

Liz remained in the cabin when Jimmy went out to the barn. He wanted her to see the bear, but to alert her he had to leave the barn and cross the open yard between it and the house. He nixed that idea pretty quickly though, thinking that going outside with nothing between himself and the bear seemed a little chancy.

One day he sat reading in the cabin loft. Happening to glance out the window, he noticed an animal traveling through tall grass in the meadow. When it exited the grass and came closer, Jimmy recognized it as a young cougar. It continued toward the cabin and approached the back porch.

What it did next surprised Jimmy. He could not believe his eyes when it ducked out of sight under the porch. He thought for a moment of going down and shining his flashlight under the porch to see what the big cat was up to.

On thinking twice however, he realized that could be a very unwise and dangerous move, so he decided to wait a while. When he went and looked under the porch the next morning, the animal had gone.

Before the cougar appeared, dozens of chipmunks played on the porch during Jimmy and Liz' earlier visits to the cabin. The 2 of them would sit in the kitchen watching the little animals out the window and laugh at their antics.

After learning of the cougar's presence, Jimmy realized they never saw any more chipmunks. From that, he guessed the chipmunks had enticed the cougar as a food source and he had eaten them, which would explain his residence under the porch and the disappearance of the chipmunks.

The wildlife, the scenic beauty and isolation of the cabin endeared it to Jimmy and Liz. They went there every summer, and sometimes in winter at Christmas time when it snowed.

They thought it a wonderful place to spend time and relax; just prop your feet up and read all day or go for walks in the mountains.

All the pleasure they derived from the cabin made it a great get-away place to relax and unwind when they needed a break from life on the farm. But the farm remained as ground zero of their normal everyday existence. Jimmy continued commuting to his practice in Ft. Walton while keeping busy in his off-time with collecting and restoring his tractors.

Liz had gotten a job with the Walton County School system, which kept her occupied during the 14 years she would spend on the farm with Jimmy.

V

≈CLOSER TO HOME≈

Selling the Ft. Walton Clinic, Practicing in De-Funiak Springs, Working with the State Prison, County Jail Doctor, Retirement and Divorce.

After practicing in Ft. Walton for 37 years, Jimmy terminated his practice there and sold the clinic in 2004. Many of those years he spent commuting between the clinic and the farm on round trips exceeding a hundred miles a day. Five Oldsmobiles gave their best years to him in the process.

By the time he sold the clinic, the government had pretty much taken over health care to the detriment of quality, in Jimmy's opinion. It had gained control through such programs as Medicare, Champus, the VA, Tricare and others so heavy with regulations that little discretion was left to doctors and their patients.

Regulations controlled when patients could be hospitalized, how long they stayed, what tests were run and what medicines they were given. That was not the best way to treat patients he believed, because bureaucrats were dictating things they should not have been.

He cited the care of heart patients as an example. On arriving at the emergency room with chest pains, the examination routinely led off with a cardiogram. If it looked normal a prompt discharge followed. The patient would go home and in the next few days, die of a heart attack.

That avoidable tragedy occurred because the doctors did not do everything they should have. Jimmy did not want to practice that way, so he closed down the clinic in 2004.

Shortly thereafter, he opened a clinic in DeFuniak Springs next to the new hospital on U. S Highway 331 just south of the I-10 exit. He practiced there for a couple of years until his accountant came to him one day and told him he knew he continued his practice just because he enjoyed it, but he had stopped making anything.

The last 5 months, the accountant told him, he made 685 dollars. Going on, the accountant told him he needed to just close the practice and stop doing it for gratification. Jimmy took his advice and closed the practice in 2006.

Some months earlier he had begun working part-time with the Walton Correctional Institution providing health care to state prison inmates. After closing the clinic, he went full-time with the prison.

When the prison initially contacted him about working for them, he hesitated at first. He told them he had his fill of government and as the state of Florida controlled the prison, he had no desire to work for them.

He rebuffed them on their first 2 calls, but on the third one they asked him not to say no, just go out and talk to them, because they wanted to make him a deal he could not refuse.

They weren't kidding. He met with them and on hearing them out, he jumped at their offer. It included terms so generous that he decided he might like working for the government after all.

They gave him full retirement benefits, which in Florida are among the most reliable in the country because the retirement system is adequately funded, 6 weeks of annual leave, 5 weeks of sick leave, health insurance and a generous salary.

He had to hire, or fire no one, he could work the hours he chose and they would send his checks directly to his bank every 2 weeks.

The prison had an infirmary, basically a hospital section where patients could be placed, just like in a hospital ward. Their complaints were evaluated and if found to be nothing serious they could be treated there.

More serious complaints, like acute appendicitis or heart attacks, for example, warranted a trip to the local hospital at tax payer expense.

As far as medicating and keeping genuinely sick patients comfortable until they recovered, that could be done just as well in the infirmary as it could in the hospital and at much less cost to tax payers.

A few years after going to work with the prison, Sheriff Ralph Johnson called Jimmy asking for his help in reducing the health care costs of inmates incarcerated in the county jail.

He spent approximately 28 thousand a month just for health care. Jimmy told him he had a full-time job taking care of inmates at the state prison and did not need anything else to do.

The Sheriff's wife worked as Jimmy's secretary at the prison. She handled all his paperwork, relieving him of that tremendous burden. She assured Jimmy the Sheriff really had a major problem dealing with his health care budget and could use his help if at all possible.

With both the sheriff and his wife double teaming him, Jimmy felt he had to try helping the Sheriff if he could. He called and told him he would go over and help out part-time, to which the Sheriff agreed.

Jimmy went over to the jail and worked when time away from the prison permitted. For 3 or 4 months he managed the prisoners' health care needs and trimmed the jail's cost from 28 to 8 thousand a month, thereby stanching the budget hemorrhage from a flood to a trickle.

He raised the level of care and reduced costs by 75 percent at the same time. That made not only the Sheriff, but also the prisoners, very happy.

During that time, the new jail under construction next to the prison neared completion, but had not advanced beyond the point where changes could still be made without substantial costs.

That gave Jimmy an opportunity to revise the plans to include an infirmary similar to the prison's which would further reduce prisoner health care costs to the Sheriff.

After completion of the new jail, Jimmy stayed on as its doctor because the infirmary enabled him to provide health care to the prisoners more efficiently and at less expense.

Making his rounds at the infirmary in the early mornings, he closely examined the sickest patients and gave the less sick a once over.

He examined lab tests, x-ray and cardiogram reports, and if he found nothing urgent, 8 a.m. or before, found him gone. If any emergencies came up after he left, he remained available to return and take care of them.

He managed to carry out his responsibilities at the jail and prison at the same time while maintaining equally high-quality healthcare at both locations which stood next door to each other.

After working at the prison for 18 years, he retired at age 78. He continued as the jail doctor for 4 more years and after serving there for a total of 16 years, he resigned at 82.

That happened in the 2017 time period and as Jimmy's working years ended, so did his time with Liz, because unbeknownst to him she had become unhappy in their marriage.

Springing it on him out of the blue; she told him she wanted a divorce. She didn't give him a reason and he didn't ask for one.

The reason being they agreed before they married that if either ever wanted out of the marriage, there would be no questions asked and they would go their separate ways amicably with neither judging the other.

It mystified Jimmy as to her reasons for wanting out because during their time together he thought they had gotten along superbly. He surmised it might have had something to do with the recent loss of her mother to Alzheimer's and her younger brother being diagnosed with the same ailment.

She seemed to need to be in Houston where her children and grandchildren lived. Possibly the pain of losing her mother and potentially, her brother as well, evoked feelings in her of needing to be closer to what biological family she had left in the event the same affliction awaited her. Jimmy could only speculate as to why because she never gave him so much as a hint.

Even though they had entered into a prenuptial agreement before they married that provided for an uncontested divorce, Liz engaged an attorney to represent her. Jimmy followed suit, but only to protect his own interest.

Assuming a punitive stance against Jimmy, Liz's attorney prepared to go to court demanding she be awarded the cabin and 171 acres in Oregon, and a $400,000 cash settlement.

But Florida law required mediation in advance of law suits going to trial. That meant the parties and their attorneys had to meet and attempt a settlement first. The suit would then go to trial only if the parties came to an impasse.

Prior to the mediation Jimmy gave Liz's attorney a copy of the prenuptial agreement, but he dismissed it, saying he could get the judge to set it aside because it did not apply.

Jimmy's attorney however took issue with that. Both parties signed the document, he told him, witnesses signed it, the parties to it had it recorded at the courthouse, making it a valid and legally binding document.

Fearing that things were about to get out of hand unnecessarily, Jimmy informed his attorney he would like to speak with Liz in private. Her attorney objected, but she told him it was her divorce, not his and she would talk to Jimmy if she wanted. Having no choice in the matter at that point, her attorney relented.

They secluded themselves in the office of Jimmy's attorney with the door closed. Jimmy asked her to tell him what she wanted and he would try to do it. He did not want to drag it out he told her, because they did not need attorneys involved.

But now they were involved and the two of them needed to settle it. Otherwise, they would end up in court for the judge to decide, he continued.

She told him she wanted to move to Houston, buy a small house and pay cash for it. Jimmy asked how much she needed and she told him 200 thousand dollars.

He wrote a check for the amount and gave it to her. "Is there anything else you need?" he asked. "No," she told him and they parted ways. They divorced after 14 years of marriage.

In telling his side of the story, he emphasized it amounted to nothing more than that; his side only. He did not know her side, so could not speak for her.

He returned to the cabin in Oregon once more after the divorce but found no pleasure in being there alone. A couple he knew had been after him for two years wanting to buy it. They offered him a nice price, so he finally called to tell them he had decided to sell and they bought it.

He flew to Pendleton to close the deal and when finished, he drove down to Bend where Polly, his flight attendant daughter lived and spent some time with she and her husband. At the end of the visit, he drove back to Pendleton to fly home from there.

Driving around the area the afternoon before he left, he happened up on a 3-story manufactured log cabin for sale. A True log structure with a heavy, steeply pitched roof on 2 acres, he immediately liked it.

He called the number on the for-sale sign, and asked the real estate lady answering the phone for the listed price. It is 220 thousand, she told him. The couple owning it wanted to retire to Arizona and if he made them a reasonable offer they might accept, she added.

He liked it so much he thought he would make them an offer. It sat on Lincton Mountain 2 miles from the cabin he had just sold but at a slightly higher elevation.

The mountain presented a spectacular view when looking up at it from the valley below. He called the real estate lady back and told her he wanted to offer 170 thousand for it. She rang him back shortly telling him the owners declined his offer, but that she told them he planned on flying out in the morning so if they wanted to accept his offer, they needed to settle it that afternoon.

Within an hour she called back telling him they had decided to accept, so he bought it.

He flew out the next morning not to return until the summer of 2019 to officially move in. He stayed 4 months and 2 days and built a new garage while there. He hired 2 licensed Mexican contractors to do the building.

He could find no one else willing to touch the project. Others he approached had projects in the valley keeping them busy. They had no desire to bother with a job on the mountain due to the hassle of getting workers, equipment and supplies up there.

How little interest they had in working on the mountain Jimmy learned from the quotes they gave him for the project. One of the two he approached quoted 71 thousand and the other wanted 67 thousand. He contracted with the Mexicans for 37 thousand.

It had to be finished before October because snow usually came by then and brought all building on the mountain to a halt.

They got it done ahead of the snow, but just barely. It wrapped up on October 15th, at 1:00 in the afternoon. Two hours later the first snowflakes fell and didn't stop for 2 nights and a day. When it finally ended 6 inches covered the ground. Jimmy locked his car and Caterpillar in the garage and caught a plane home to Florida.

During his stay at the cabin in 2019, Penny spent 3 weeks with him, a visit they both very much enjoyed. In 2021, she again accompanied him to the cabin and plans to remain indefinitely. She has taken on the project of completing the guest quarters on the second floor of the garage. When complete, it will be a fully equipped apartment suitable for long term occupancy.

VI

≈WHEEL TRACTORS≈

Ray Barrow, Overview and John Deere Tractors.

Jimmy began restoring tractors in earnest about 1994 at age 60. The same year he became acquainted with Ray Barrow of Holt, Florida. Ray had retired in his late 50s from his job as a mechanic because of a disability. An accident involving a ruptured high pressure hydraulic hose injured the fingers on his right hand so severely as to disable him from doing his work.

At the time Jimmy met him however, his fingers had healed sufficiently to permit him to return to mechanic work although still partially disabled.

When Ray learned of Jimmy's interest in restoring old tractors, the 2 of them became fast friends. As a long-time mechanic, Ray loved that line of work and volunteered to assist Jimmy in his endeavors.

His disability retirement benefits provided him with an adequate income unsupplemented by gainful employment. With nothing else to fill his time, he happily assisted Jimmy with the satisfaction in rejuvenating worn-out old machines to like-new condition as his only pay.

He and Jimmy worked as a team with Ray performing those tasks not requiring precision manual dexterity and Jimmy doing those that did. Ray compensated for his loss of dexterity with the use of pneumatic impact tools as long as the job at hand permitted, such as there being sufficient room to apply the tools.

In places where bolts and nuts needed removing or installing but limited space prevented the use of impact tools, only the nimble deftness of Jimmy's fingers could efficiently accomplish the task in minutes whereas Ray fumbled with it, sometimes for hours.

By dividing their abilities along those lines, work on any given project proceeded smoothly to completion, depending of course, on whether they had the necessary parts and supplies on hand.

Procuring those parts and supplies, as well as finding tractors to restore, fell almost exclusively to Jimmy. Over the many years of indulging his hobby, he networked with others across the country who shared the same interest. When in need of a particular part, he first queried those contacts in connection with the item he sought.

If that proved unsuccessful, as it sometimes did, he added the item to his wish list of parts needed that he would look for on his next outing in search of restorable tractors. In a few instances, it took him as many as 10 years before he found what he needed. In the meantime, he set that project aside and proceeded with others in various stages of restoration, of which he had more than enough to keep Ray and himself occupied.

As he gained experience in his restorations, he learned early on that it cost no more to restore a rare tractor than it did a more common one. He read everything he could find on John Deere tractors to inform himself of the rarest models and what made them so.

Typically, it depended on the number of a particular model built. John Deere built a large number of some models, but a very small number of others. A specimen from a small production run is therefore, rarer and more valuable than one from a larger production run.

Jimmy acquainted himself with the rarest models and when he found one, that knowledge usually gave him the advantage in bargaining with the owner who rarely ever knew its true worth.

More often than not, the owner snapped up Jimmy's offer of a few hundred dollars, believing he had put one over on him by unloading what he considered a piece of junk for much more than he thought it to be worth. Jimmy still laughs at those, of which there were many.

On occasion, he received a tip on a rare tractor for sale that he wanted, but for one reason or another, failed to get there before another collector beat him to it.

He recalled one such instance when a friend in West Virginia called him about a rare John Deere model 62 the owner wanted to sell for 25 hundred dollars, but Jimmy knew its actual worth to be somewhere in the range of 20 thousand dollars.

A controversy surrounding that particular model arose over whether the factory intended it as an experimental version leading up to the L model production tractor, or, if instead, its development never went beyond the experimental stage. The controversy hung in limbo because the factory never clarified the matter.

Jimmy asked his friend to put a 5-hundred-dollar binder on the tractor with its serial number written on the check. Then, when he went to pick it up, he would pay the owner the balance due. His friend however, told him no binder would be necessary because when he went to pick it up it would be there.

Jimmy argued the point with him, fearing that without a binder, the owner would sell the tractor to the first person that showed up with the cash to buy it.

The friend told him no, he had known the owner since their childhood days and he trusted him. Further, he guaranteed Jimmy the owner would not sell it to anyone else.

Contrary to Jimmy's wishes, the friend never put a binder on the tractor. When Jimmy called the owner a few days later to let him know he planned on going to pick it up, the man told him he had sold the tractor to someone else. Jimmy never let his friend live that one down.

Jimmy learned on another occasion that even when he gave the seller a check in full payment of the agreed-on purchase price for a tractor, it did not guarantee he would get the tractor -- or his money back, for that matter.

That happened when he found a rare tractor in Wisconsin he wanted to buy. He gave the owner (a Mr. X, for purposes of this story) a check with the serial number written on it, in full payment of the tractor.

When Jimmy later sent his truck to pick up the tractor, Mr. X had sold it to someone else for a higher price. In the meantime, Mr. X cashed Jimmy's check and spent the money, giving Jimmy that excuse for not returning it when he called asking for his money back.

Jimmy decided that suing him would be pointless because it would cost him more than he paid for the tractor, so he wrote it off as a loss. He later learned from other collectors of Mr. X's reputation as a notorious scammer. Unfortunately, Jimmy learned it too late to prevent himself from being cheated.

The time came however, when Jimmy had the opportunity to scam Mr. X back. A fellow collector friend of Jimmy's named Jim Zimmerman had a place in Orchard, Iowa. On a trip to Zimmerman's to pick up a tractor he bought; Jimmy spotted another tractor sitting on the property he knew to be rare. He could hardly believe his ears when Zimmerman told him the tractor belonged to Mr. X.

That set wheels turning in Jimmy's head and he asked Zimmerman if he had anything tied up in the tractor. Zimmerman replied no, it awaited a truck he expected to pick it up for delivery to Mr. X.

After filling Zimmerman in on his sorry experience with Mr. X, Jimmy backed up his truck to the tractor, loaded it and took it home with him. When Mr. X called to complain, Jimmy reminded him of the stunt he pulled on him. Further, Jimmy told him when he scammed others, he should expect the same in return.

Jimmy also learned where the best tractors for restoring could be found. It depended on the climate and how well the owners cared for their machines. Southern farmers he learned, too often left their tractors to the mercy of the elements.

They seldom bothered to protect them from too frequent rain and the harmful effects of the sun on the paint. Those factors in addition to the high humidity of southern weather tended to break down the paint and lead to premature rusting of the metal.

Neither did they properly maintain the tractors by adequately lubricating them against excessive wear and keeping them free of dirt and trash which held rust inducing moisture against the metal they coated.

Due to these conditions, tractors aged 40, 50 and 60 years or more sitting out in the weather on southern farms remained little more than rusted hulks beyond any hope of restoration.

The same could not be said however, of old tractors found in the Midwest and western parts of the country. Both the lower humidity and less abundant rain in those regions reduced the atmospheric moisture associated with the rusting problems experienced in the south.

Additionally, farmers better protected the valuable assets their tractors represented by sheltering them from the weather and keeping them properly maintained and serviced against excessive wear and tear.

When those farmers retired their old tractors and moved them out of the barn to make way for new ones, the old machines remained in much better shape to endure the ravages they suffered from decades of outdoor exposure considerably less wearing on them than in the south.

They became the candidates most sought after by Jimmy and his fellow collectors for restoration and they make up the bulk of Jimmy's collection.

To be more conveniently situated in assisting Jimmy with his restorations, Ray Barrow relocated from his former home in Holt to a house located near Jimmy's farm.

He remained with Jimmy for about 25 years, in which time he did the bulk of the mechanical work on approximately 85 percent of the hundred or so tractors they returned to like-new condition during that period.

Health issues related to strokes both Ray and his wife suffered forced them to go live with their children in Santa Rosa County, ending Ray's many years of work with Jimmy about 2018.

Narrative descriptions of selected tractors from Jimmy's collection follow. Included in the narratives are cross references to photos of each tractor found in the photos section.

Jimmy believes these to be among the rarest of his John Deere wheel tractor group. What makes each one significant is explained in the narratives. All tractor photos were made and copyrighted by the author.

No. 1 (p. 223), No. 1 View A and B, is the 1924 John Deere model N, Waterloo Boy tractor, SN 29583, in Jimmy's collection. The Waterloo Gas Engine Company of Waterloo, Iowa, produced the model R, predecessor of the

N, from 1914 to 1917, based on designs of John Froelich who organized the Company in 1895.

In 1917, the Company came out with the Model N. Both models proved highly successful in the farm tractor market, equally in America and Great Britain during WWI. So much so that they caught the attention of Deere & Company, who sought a successful farm tractor with which they could enter that market.

In 1918, Deere & Co. purchased the Waterloo Company and took over production of its tractors. Deere however, continued selling the tractors under the Waterloo Boy name until 1924, when they ended its production in October of that year.

They replaced it with the John Deere Model D, famously known as the "Spoker D," after its unique spoked flywheel. It entered the market as the first tractor built under the John Deere name.

The Waterloo Boy is one of his tractors Jimmy did not restore himself. He purchased it from the late Robert Schreiber who bought the tractor in Canada. Kenneth J. Kass (1949-2021), of Dunkerton, Iowa, did the restoration work on it.

Because of the near pristine condition to which Kass restored it, the John Deere Company borrowed it from Jimmy to exhibit at the Company's 150th anniversary celebration in Waterloo, Iowa which took place on the 16th through 19th of July, 1987.

The tractor runs on kerosene, but requires a dose of gasoline to start. Its radiator is turned sideways, as noted in view B. The hand crank, visible on the left side of the photo in View A, is used to start the engine. Once started and put in motion, it creeps along at the walking speed of about 3 miles per hour.

When the State of Nebraska set up the tractor testing program at the University of Nebraska in 1920 to establish uniform quality and performance standards for farm tractors manufactured in the United States, the Waterloo Boy N became the first tractor to pass the test.

The tractor is rare and Jimmy believes it to be arguably the most valuable of the tractors in his John Deere collection.

No. 2 (p. 224). This 1924 John Deere Model D., or "Spoker D," as it became popularly known, derived that nickname from its spoked flywheel. (See next to rear wheel in the referenced photo). Originally 26 inches in diameter, the flywheel shrunk to 24 inches in 1925 on learning the larger wheel tended to contact the back edge of the left front wheel when it rolled over an elevated spot of ground in a maximum left-turn position.

Metal wheels were standard for tractors at the time and rubber tires would not replace them for a few more years after the Model D rolled out of the factory.

A unique feature of the tractor in addition to the spoked flywheel is its cast iron seat with the letters "Deere & Co." cut out in the metal. John Deere introduced it as the first tractor bearing the company name.

Although the history of Jimmy's Spoker D that follows indicates the Waterloo Gasoline Engine Co. built the tractor, that is incorrect. The John Deere Tractor Company built it at the former Waterloo Boy factor in Waterloo, Iowa. It succeeded the Waterloo Boy, which launched John Deere into the farm tractor business.

This fully restored vintage tractor is rare in its own right due to the model's scarcity. Its value is greatly enhanced also by its documented history as follows:

JOHN DEERE MODEL "D" TRACTOR

No. 34331	Weight, 4164 Dry
Bore 6-1/2"	Speed, 800 RPM
Stroke 7"	H. P. Draw-Bar 16
	Belt 27

This tractor was built by the Waterloo Gasoline Engine company, Waterloo, Iowa, 20 August 1925. It was shipped to the John Deere Plow Company, Milwaukee, Wisconsin, on 21 August 1925.

It was bought along with a John Deere, No. 5, 3-bottom 14" plow at the Wisconsin State Fair in September 1925, by Adam Ebling, who lived near Richfield, Wisconsin. It then worked plowing, threshing, pulling a 28" Case separator and clover hulling, accumulating approximately 30,000 hours of operation having been rebored 3 times to the maximum of .125 oversize. The tractor was driven to the apple orchard in back of the Ebling farm and was last run in 1951.

In 1966, the writer found the tractor, as shown in the picture, with the help of his late good friend, J. Ally Schuster of Goldendale, Wisconsin. The tractor was bought from the son, Albert J. Ebling in September 1966. It was restored in the winter of 1966-67 to its original condition.

Some interesting facts about the John Deere "Model D" are:

1. It has an open or spoke-type flywheel, and a cast iron crankcase and transmission cover with cast raised letters, "Waterloo Gasoline Engine Co., Waterloo Iowa, U. S. A."
2. There were 5849 tractors built quipped with the open-spoke-type flywheel.
3. The first spoke type bore Serial Number 30400 and was built December 24, 1923.
4. The John Deere Company bought out the Waterloo Engine Company in 1917 and built the Waterloo Boy Tractor until the famous John Deere "D" came out in 1923.
5. The same rugged simple basic design of the famous John Deere "D" was built from 1923 to 1949 which certainly is a credit to this great tractor and its designers.

Lee J. Wanie
Horicon, Wisconsin

A feature the writer failed to mention is the tractor's cast iron steering wheel, which is rare. In listing his "interesting facts" about the tractor, the writer omitted the high number of injuries operators suffered from getting hands and arms caught in the spokes when manually spinning the flywheel to start the tractor.

To eliminate the hazard, the company in 1926 replaced the spoked wheel with a solid disc type found on later model tractors. The writer also noted the Model D remained in production from 1923 to 1949, a period of 26 years. Another source, however, claims its production spanned 30 years, from 1923 to 1953, which set a record no other John Deere tractor has matched.

Note that Lee Wanie, in his foregoing history of the tractor, writes that "It was restored to its original condition." He did not specify however, what the restoration entailed. The tractor eventually found its way to a collector in South Florida, from whom Jimmy acquired it.

He stated that when it came into his possession, it had been painted, but otherwise not restored. He undertook the work needed in completing the restoration himself to bring the tractor to its like-new condition, both internally and externally, as it appears in the accompanying photo.

No. 3 (p. 224), is a 1932 GPO (General Purpose Orchard) tractor. Some sources report the production period of this tractor as 1928 through 1935. The tractors came from the factory with all steel wheels but they could be replaced with rubber tires purchased at the owner's expense. Only about 717 of the GPOs were built, making them rare.

The tractor's low profile and fendered rear wheels met the special needs of orchard owners for a tractor that easily passed underneath trees with the fenders protecting over hanging branches from damage by the large rear wheels.

Jimmy found this tractor in Summerville, Oregon. The previous owner, a skilled mechanic, had completely restored it; including the engine, transmission, carburetor, magneto, and all cosmetics. The tractor originally came with steel wheels, but the previous owner had ordered rubber tires as replacements for them. Jimmy sold the steel wheels for about 8 hundred dollars.

No. 4 (p. 225) is a 1933 John Deere GP (General Purpose), Wide-Tread, tractor, "unstyled." It features a top steering ("over the top") mechanism and wide gauge rear wheels with factory round spokes, all of which are rare.

The rear axle spans 76 inches and the front wheels are tricycle. It also features a magneto that can be retarded or advanced as needed to improve engine performance. This predated later tractors fitted with distributors which could be similarly advanced or retarded by setting the timing.

This is the rarest of the GP model series with less than 500 of them produced. A custom fabricator in Iowa built and painted the hood and silk screened the John Deere decals on it.

Jimmy acquired the tractor through a friend, the late Robert Schreiber, of Iowa who had done some restoration on it. But after Jimmy bought it, he and Ray Barrow finished the remaining restoration work it needed in returning it to like-new condition.

No. 5 (p. 225) is a 1934 A, dual rear wheels, factory round spokes, brass tag, unstyled, rare. The brass tag signifies the tractor included in first year model production. Dual rear wheels with factory round spokes; rare. John Deere introduced the A as its first true row-crop model replacing the GP (General Purpose) and its first with factory installed rubber tires.

Jimmy thinks he found it somewhere in the midwestern U. S. between 1975-90. In clean condition when he bought it, but carburetor and magneto required rebuilding. Balance of restoration included a new paint job and decals. Jimmy and Ray Barrow restored it.

No. 6 (p. 226) is a 1935 BN (Model B, N-narrow, for single front wheel). Unstyled. It is early production as evidenced by the 4-bolt pedestal, which the company produced as the Garden B until serial number 1803 in 1935.

Beginning with that serial number, 8 bolts attached the pedestal to the frame after which the company designated the tractor as the Model BN. Its Factory flat spoke rear wheels are rare. Has early PTO driven lift with the letter "B" imprinted on casting cover.

John Deere produced only 24 Garden Bs, making it rare due to the small number built. The number remaining in existence after the 87 years between 1935 and 2022 is unknown, but is likely even smaller, making it extremely rare. Jimmy looked for a tractor of this model for about 15 years before finding it in Iowa. He restored it himself.

No 7 (p. 226) is a 1937 John Deere AOS (model A, Orchard, Streamlined), "styled," a very early production tractor. It numbered 57th in the sequence of those produced, although the total number built is unknown.

Grove operators towed equipment that sprayed orchards with toxic chemicals for insect and disease control behind this tractor. The chemicals so badly corroded its sheet metal that it hung on the tractor in tatters when it came to Jimmy.

The owner of the tractor brought it from western Oregon to an auction in Clear Water, Florida. The auctioneer announced a 15% charge to sellers. When he began the auction, he went from one tractor to another without receiving any bids.

When he came to this tractor, Jimmy bid 5 hundred on it. Someone else bid 550. Jimmy countered with 6 hundred and no other bids followed, leaving him with the highest bid. He thought it to be worth about 25 hundred dollars.

It took him 10 years to get all the sheet metal fabricated to restore it. He could not find a single fabricator to do all the metal, but had to piece it out to 3 different ones. That resulted in the separate parts not fitting together satisfactorily when he tried installing them on the tractor.

He called on his friend, Leonard Thomas, who managed the body shop for the Chevrolet dealership in Geneva, Alabama, to help him solve that problem. With more than 30 years of experience in auto body work, Leonard did a masterful job of coaxing the metal together so seamlessly as to give it the look of a factory job.

187

No. 8 (p. 227) is a John Deere 1938 Model A, Wide, High, or AWH. "Wide" is in reference to its widely spaced front wheel as opposed to a tricycle front end.

"High" means its axles and chassis clear the ground at a greater height than the average tractor, making it suitable for use on crops which lower clearance tractors might damage.

It is an unstyled model, of which the company built approximately 48, making it extremely rare and highly sought after by collectors.

The small number manufactured mostly went to vegetable growers in California, the only farmers in the country doing well enough during the depression to afford new tractors.

Jimmy found the tractor in California and sold it to an individual in South Carolina who restored it. He had no desire to keep it however, and Jimmy bought it back from him.

No. 9 (p. 227) is a 1938 John Deere BI (Model B, Industrial), tractor. It is a departure from agricultural tractors in that these machines were typically painted yellow for better visibility when used on highways, roads and construction sites. The factory built approximately 91 of them, making this tractor extremely rare.

It has an upholstered seat, emergency brake lever and a cast front designed for mounting implements such as street sweepers and mowers for road-side grass cutting.

There is an anecdote behind how Jimmy came by this tractor. He and two collector friends; Kent Kaster and Carl

Montgomery, were headed to a tractor swap-meet in Indiana. The friends told him they knew a collector who owned the only 2 rare 1938 BI tractors in the state of Indiana and if he would like to see them, they could stop by his place which they would pass along the way.

Jimmy told them he would like to see the tractors but before they arrived the friends told him not to bother asking to buy one of them because they had both already asked and were turned down.

When they arrived at the collector's place, Jimmy saw that one of the tractors had been restored but the other had not. In spite of being advised against it, Jimmy decided, what the heck, he would ask the guy if he wanted to sell the unrestored tractor anyway.

To his surprise, and that of his friends, the man agreed to sell him the tractor. Jimmy gave him a check to bind the sale and made arrangements to pick it up at a later date.

As they continued on their trip to the swap-meet, the two friends wondered out loud as to why the man sold Jimmy the tractor after he had refused to sell it to either of them. In the absence of an answer, they could only shake their heads as to the reason.

When Jimmy returned a week or so later to pick up the tractor, he asked the man that burning question and had to laugh at the answer. The man sold him the tractor, he said, because he lived in Florida.

He would take it out of Indiana, leaving himself as the owner of the only rare tractor of its kind in the entirety of that state. Understanding the full implications of that, Jimmy found his logic both impeccable and amusing at the same time.

No. 10 (p. 228), is a 1938 G, Unstyled. Big radiator. First year production, cast Iron PTO cover, all rare features. Factory dual round spoked rear wheels, very rare. Front Goodyear tires, rare.

This tractor came about as a remedy for the overheating problems of its predecessor Model G, low radiator tractor. Due to a radiator sized too small to adequately cool the engine, the tractor tended to run hot during extended usage under heavy load conditions.

When owners of the tractor complained about the overheating problem to John Deere dealers, they dispatched a truck to the farm and replaced the low radiators with larger ones on site. Other components replaced included the fuel tank and hood, which required larger sizes to accommodate the bigger radiator. The dealers made the modifications at no cost to the owners.

Due to the overheating issue, the company ended production of the low radiator model with serial number 4250. The first large radiator production model replacing it began with serial number 4251 and continued until the company stopped making that version of the G. The dual rear wheels came as an optional upgrade over the single rear wheels of the model G.

The Good Year tires on the front wheels are rare due to their unusual design. Instead of treads with a level cross-section as with most tires, these are beveled so the outward leaning tires sit flat on the ground. This makes them more durable than normal tires which would wear more heavily on the edge in contact with the ground at an angle.

Kent Kaster of Shelbyville, Indiana, originally collected this tractor. Jimmy bought it from him and he and Ray Barrow restored it.

No. 11 (p. 228), is a 1938 Model G, Low radiator, unstyled. First year production. Factory round spoke wheels. Very rare. Although engineering specs indicated the engine would run at peak efficiency with its small coolant capacity, experience in the field proved otherwise.

After many of the tractors suffered overheating problems, the company issued a recall. The fix required a radiator with increased coolant capacity, as well as a larger fuel tank and hood to accommodate the upsized radiator. Dealers made the modifications on site at no expense to the owners.

Due to the overheating issue plaguing the tractor, the company replaced it with a succeeding model designed with an adequate cooling system (beginning with serial number 4251). Many of the "big radiator" varieties of the model as shown in photo No. 10, were dealer conversions.

Jimmy bought this tractor in California. The man who owned it said it never ran hot with him so he never had the radiator changed out as others did. Jimmy and Ray Barrow restored it.

No. 12 (p. 229), is a 1950 John Deere model MTW, with the W meaning "Wide front axle," as differentiated from the same model with a more common tricycle configuration.

It is the only tractor John Deere built with a telescoping steering column. It is identical to the one the Sheppards traded their model LA in on except theirs had the tricycle front axle much more popular with farmers because it could "turn on a dime."

The wide front axle model could not match the tricycle version in maneuverability, making it less popular with farmers. Its wide front stance however, had greater stability on slopes and when fitted with a front-end loader doing heavy work.

Its lower demand led to fewer sales, which in turn, disincentivized its production to the point it became rare in terms of its collectible value. To Jimmy, it also has sentimental value because of its similarity to the second tractor he had on the farm as a boy.

Jimmy's friend, the late Robert Schreiber (1923-2014), of Milo, Iowa, alerted him to this tractor. He called Jimmy, telling him the tractor belonged to a neighbor who had recently died and his widow wanted to sell it for 25 hundred dollars.

The owner bought it new about 45 years prior to his death. He kept it sheltered, cleaned and serviced it regularly and it looked brand new. Jimmy thought it a bargain at the price asked and sent Schreiber the money to buy it. Long familiar with this tractor as a tricycle, Jimmy never knew it also came in wide fronts until many years after he began collecting tractors.

No. 13 (p. 229), is a 1942 John Deere Model H. It has every available feature John Deere offered on this model tractor. Included are dual lights, electric starter, hydraulic powered cultivator lift, rear fenders and PTO.

The steering wheel can be removed and mated to the flywheel hub for manual starting when the electric start fails. It has cast iron front wheel rims, and louvered radiator shutters for heat regulation, with the control mounted on the dash within easy reach of the driver.

The tall engine air intake tube protruding vertically from the hood on other tractors disappeared from this one. In its place, the engine breathes through an intake opening cut in the left side of the hood ducted to an under-the-hood oil-bath air cleaner arrangement.

Jimmy does not recall where he got the tractor, but it sat in his barn for 25 years before he decided to restore it. Not knowing if it would even run, he asked his friend and fellow tractor restorer, Charles Kinky, to help him try starting it.

In the absence of a battery to power the electric starter they had to start it manually. To do that, Charles mounted the steering wheel to the flywheel so he could turn the engine over.

After only a few turns with the liberal use of starting fluid, the engine fired off and ran smoothly. Hearing it run so well, Jimmy decided to go ahead and restore it. He asked

Charles if he would take it to his shop and do the work for him, to which Charles agreed.

Sometime later he brought it back restored to like-new condition. Jimmy settled with him for the work in the amount of about 3 thousand dollars.

Jimmy stated that in his travels across the country, he has never seen another model H with all the features this one has, which makes it very rare.

No. 14 (p. 230) is a 1959, 830-I (Industrial) diesel, 2-cylinder John Deere with power steering. About 2 thousand model 830s were built. Only about 50 were industrial models, so this tractor is rare.

Jimmy is not certain where he found the tractor, but thinks it came from a farmer in Dawn, Iowa, whom he paid 3 thousand dollars for it, which he considered "top dollar." He and Ray Barrow restored it.

No. 15 (p. 230), is a 1959-60 John Deere 840-I, (Industrial). Very rare, approximately 25 to 30 built. Largest 2-cylinder diesel John Deere engine built. Vertical 1,000 RPM PTO. Offset driver position. Pulls original 8-yard dirt pan which Jimmy also owns. Dirt pan is self-loading and unloading.

J. E. Hancock owner of Hancock Manufacturing Company, Lubbock, Texas, manufactured the Hancock 7E2 scraper, which he sold from his John Deere dealership in Lubbock. In 1958, he established the Yellowhouse Machinery Company, the only John Deere Dealership in the region selling John Deere construction equipment exclusively.

Also in 1958, Hancock contracted with John Deere to produce the 840I, a beefed-up version of the John Deere 830I, intended as the tow machine for his scraper. He produced the tractor from October 1958 to February 1959, during which he built 63 of them.

But when he failed to meet John Deere's desired production numbers as well as their quality control standards Deere discontinued the contract and took over production of the tractor. They upgraded it with a number of improvements aimed at better durability, performance and serviceability.

To differentiate it from the Hancock built versions, John Deere dubbed it the "New Style." Making no changes in marketing the tractor, they continued selling it as a package with the John Deere scraper as originally intended.

The model year of Jimmy's 840I is dated after John Deere took over its production, an indication it is one of the "New Style," models postdating those built by Hancock.

Jimmy found the tractor in southern California. He and Ray Barrow restored it.

VII

≈CRAWLER TRACTORS≈

Collection Strategy, Caterpillar and its Predecessors and Review of Selected Crawler Tractors.

When deciding to expand his collection efforts into crawler tractors, Jimmy followed the same strategy used with his wheel tractors. As he had learned from his John Deere experience, rare crawlers could sometimes, but not always, be obtained just as cheaply as common ones. But the restoration cost between the two usually differed very little.

In that knowledge, he researched crawlers to determine which were the rarest and where best to find them. As to the rarest, he learned those to be, with few exceptions, the early machines produced by the companies leading to the modern Caterpillar crawler, principally Best and Holt.

Those companies rose to prominence in California, which along with other west coast states, became the leading domestic U. S. market area for crawler tractor manufacturers.

As he had learned with wheel tractors, old retired crawlers left sitting out in the semi-arid weather of

California collected less rust than those in more humid parts of the country.

He also learned that owners of old crawler tractors knew no more about the value of their machines than did owners of old wheel tractors, regardless of where in the country they lived.

So, California became the destination of choice for collectors of vintage crawler tractors, because they were plentiful, generally in good condition and cheap. Jimmy found that to be true when he travelled there in search of old crawlers himself and it was where he found 2 of his most valuable antique track machines, both built by Best.

The history of the modern crawler tractor in the U. S. began with two men; Daniel Best and Benjamin Holt. Best hailed from Ohio and Holt from New Hampshire. As young men, they both migrated to California and began experimenting with agricultural machinery.

Working independently and unaware of each other in the beginning, they paralleled each other in creating machines similar in design and purpose. Their first major inventions were horse-drawn combine grain harvesters.

The successful marketing of those machines established them securely in the agricultural equipment manufacturing industry. Best established and headed the Best Manufacturing Company in San Leandro, California, about 1886.

Benjamin Holt headed the Holt Manufacturing Company located in Stockton, California, which he and his 3 brothers established in 1883.

Due to the growth in size and complexity of the machines they built, the power required in operating them far exceeded the ability of horse teams to provide. That set both men on separate paths in developing machines that could provide the power they needed.

Steam powered tractors, known as traction machines, began generating considerable interest at the time. Best and Holt saw them as possible solutions to their power needs and undertook efforts to improve and adapt them to their uses.

Each of them built improved and advanced versions of the steam tractor. A pivotal point in improving the steam tractor came with the replacement of wheels by crawler tracks as a means of locomotion.

The concept first appeared in England in 1825. Over the next 30 or so years, efforts at building a practical crawler design failed until 1858 when a steam tractor equipped as a crawler appeared in a California fair, but nothing came of it.

The concept next appeared in 1900 on steam powered crawler tractors built by Alex Lombard for logging in Maine. After seeing one of Lombard's machines, Benjamin Holt set out to adapt tracks to his steam tractors because of their superior performance on soft ground compared to wheels.

The tracks on Holt's machine gave rise to the name Caterpillar in 1905. When the company photographer saw the machine in motion, he remarked that the undulating tracks moved like a big caterpillar. Holt registered the name as the company trademark in 1910.

But tracks alone could not redeem the steam tractor. They were too large, heavy and poorly maneuverable to be practical. For several decades however, they remained the next best option to horses in providing motive power to large agricultural machines.

Recognizing the limits of steam power, both men turned their attention to gas powered internal combustion engines. The ensuing race to perfect gas-powered crawler tractors pitted them against each other as competitors in quest of some future ideal machine, the final form of which neither had an inkling.

It seemed that with every new innovation one brought out, the other quickly matched. That led to allegations of patent infringement, followed by law suits.

The suits flew back and forth between them like tennis balls with neither gaining the advantage until 1908. That year, Holt gained the upper hand in an agreement to settle out of court with Best in a suit that had drug on since 1905.

It ended with Daniel Best selling two-thirds of his company to Holt, and giving the remaining third to his son, Clarence Leo, aka C. L., who under terms of the agreement, became company president. Having lost his company, Daniel went into retirement.

C. L. remained as president for a couple of years. But the Holt board of directors who held the controlling interest in the business, frustrated his efforts at accomplishing anything.

Deciding he would be happier without them, he left in 1910 to form his own company, which he established as the C. L. Best Gas Traction Company near his father's old plant in San Leandro. Holt sued again, alleging breach of contract, but lost.

In 1912, C. L. came out with his first crawler, which he called a Tracklayer. In 1915, Holt brought suit, again alleging patent infringement. But C. L. turned the tables on them in a masterful gambit.

Holt's track design he used on his steam tractors and later his Caterpillars copied the design of Alvin Lombard's 1900 steam traction logger tracks. When C. L. learned that Lombard's patented design predated Holts, he bought the patent from Lombard.

He then countersued Holt for patent infringement, forcing them to settle on his terms. Advantage C. L. Although not the only award he won in the settlement, the right to use Holt's track design on his tracklayers proved the most important because it left him in a stronger position to compete with Holt.

The companies continued competing with new innovations and in 1914, both came out with machines minus the tiller wheels common on all crawlers up to that time. Previously, crawlers relied on the front mounted tiller wheel for steering. It allowed the operator to drive the tractor with a steering wheel like an automobile.

But that changed with the 1914 Holt Caterpillar 45 and Best Tracklayer 40 of the same year. They both used a lever controlled clutching system for steering, which rendered the tiller wheel obsolete. That innovation represented a major advancement in the design of crawler tractors in that they became more compact with greater maneuverability.

Holt took the Caterpillar to the battlefield when WWI broke out in Europe. Most of the company's production went to the military over the duration of the war for use in towing heavy artillery and supply trains across rugged terrain.

The approximately 10 thousand machines Holt sent to Europe would come back to bite them when the war ended. The company overexpanded its production capacity in relation to the number of tractors sold, which left it holding a huge debt load when hostilities ended.

Many of the tractors going to Europe with the military came back home to the U. S. as cheap surplus after the Army no longer needed them. Holt then found its new tractors in competition with those cheap machines in the domestic market, causing sales of new crawlers to drop precipitously. Benjamin Holt died in 1920 with the threat of bankruptcy looming.

Best missed out on military contracts during the war, but considering Holt's situation afterwards, that may have saved him from ending up as Holt did. He persuaded the government against restricting his supply of steel in wartime below what he needed to continue building tractors for American farmers.

His tractors sold well in the domestic market during the war, plus he had avoided incurring significant debt. With his former competitor all but eliminated, he had the market all to himself and unlike Holt, his future looked bright.

The popularity of his new Best 60 Tracklayer introduced in 1919 also bode well for the company's future. "It was to become the best-known of all of C. L. Best's tractors, and was the finest large tractor then made." In 1921, he followed the "60" with the Best 30 Tracklayer. Like its big brother, the "30" "met huge approval in the marketplace."

Sometime prior to 1925, representatives of the Holt Company approached Best about the possibility of a merger of the 2 companies. Stock holders of both companies liked the idea and the merger became a reality on April 15, 1925 with incorporation of the Caterpillar Tractor Company.

C. L. became chairman of the board and the company named the Best factory in San Leandro as its new headquarters and production facility. Its planned production runs were limited to only 5 models.

Jimmy's antique crawler collection includes all 5 of them, of which his Holt 10 Ton, and the Best 60 and 30 Tracklayers are featured herein. Narratives describing each of the tractors follow. Their photos, made and copyrighted by the author, as well as those of a selection of 8 rare Caterpillars, are presented in the photos section as cross referenced in the narratives.

No. 1 (p. 231), is a 1925 C. L. Best 60 Logging Cruiser, Serial Number A2654. Only about 1% of Best 60s were loggers. Jimmy believes it to be the only one known to exist. It has a top mounted seat, fold-down buggy top, original brass lights, gear driven generator, a temperature gage in the radiator cap and the red track pads are new.

It is equipped with a logging package and includes a high-speed 3rd gear. It has cast idler bolt covers, a front tow hook and a heavy radiator guard.

The upright red cylindrical container in the foreground is the original oiling pot that came with every new Best 60 tractor, but as far as Jimmy knows, it is not the one coming with his tractor when it was new.

Jimmy found the tractor about 1990 in Sutter Creek, California. He and a collector friend, the late Bill Santos (1926-2014), were driving back roads looking for old tractors. They saw this one sitting in weeds behind an old barn, but not having identified the property owner, thought it better to do so and obtain permission before venturing onto the site.

They drove around the neighborhood looking for someone who might direct them to the owner. Finally, a man they came up on pointed out to them the home of the person they sought.

They stopped at the house and when they asked the man answering the door if he wanted to sell the tractor, although he seemed surprised that anyone might be interested in it, he said yes.

He told them he had wanted to get it hauled off for junk. But getting it hauled would cost him 4 hundred dollars and the junkyard would only pay him 3 hundred for it, netting him a hundred-dollar loss. Rather than do that, he told them, he would just let it sit there and rust.

He gave them permission to go look at the tractor, but did not accompany them. When they got close enough to see it clear of the weeds, something about it struck Jimmy as peculiar. It displayed a Caterpillar radiator, but certain other features he noted suggested it to be older than a tractor of that make.

Although the inspection plates, of which there were two on each side of the engine, had nothing printed on them identifying it as anything other than a Caterpillar, he immediately recognized the four-knobbed fasteners securing the inspection cover plates to the hind gear housing as belonging to a Best tractor, whereas Caterpillar fasteners had only 3 knobs.

That sent him in search of the serial plate which would positively identify the make. Using his pocket knife, he poked around in the thick, decades old layers of black paint covering the area where he knew the serial plate to be and finally located it. Its location, more than anything printed on it confirmed for him the tractor's make. Although the plate showed the serial number, it did not bear the name "Best."

He knew however, that the serial plate on every Best-60 he had ever seen, of which there were many, always had its serial plate positioned near the front of the frame, on the side below the bottom-left corner of the radiator. No Caterpillar he had ever seen carried a similar plate mounted in the same place. The location of the plate convinced him he had found a Best-60.

That raised considerably his and Bill's interest in the machine. After cranking it over to ensure the engine had not seized, which it had not, they agreed that Bill would buy it.

Jimmy did not recall the amount paid, but thought it to be very little in view of the owner's plans to scrap it.

Bill had it transported to his shop in Newcastle where he went to work on it. He made the repairs necessary to get the engine running, which Jimmy remained long enough to observe, then returned home to Florida. Bill replaced the blank inspection plates with replicas of the originals bearing the Best name printed on them.

As a template for his replicas, he borrowed one of the inspection plates from an agricultural model Best 60 with 4 intact originals, owned by Fred Heidrick Sr. of Woodland, CA.

Taking it to the Knight Foundry, a water-powered foundry and machine shop in operation since 1873 in Sutter Creek, he soon had 4 brand new Best labeled inspection plates for his tractor, thanks to the shop's fabrication expertise.

He returned Heidrick's plate to them and took the new ones and mounted them on his tractor. Bill also found one of the original cast aluminum magneto covers for it. After he finished fixing it up, the tractor ran reasonably well and seemed in good condition, both mechanically and cosmetically.

Believing it to be an excellent candidate for restoration, Jimmy bought the tractor from Bill for 6 thousand dollars. At anything under 10 thousand dollars Jimmy knew it to be a steal, so he got it at a bargain.

When Jimmy picked the tractor up for transport back to Florida, its Caterpillar radiator still needed changing out with one bearing the correct tractor name. He found the Best named replacement he needed on a Caterpillar 60 in Spokane, Washington and bought it, tractor and all.

He shipped the machine the 36 hundred miles from Spokane to Florida, swapped radiators between it and his Best 60, and sold the "Cat," which was a logger, to a man in California.

In the end, he spent more hauling the Caterpillar back and forth across the country than he sold it for, but he finally had a genuine all original, Best-60 logging cruiser, right down to the brass priming cup on top of the vacuum gas pump.

It needed gas to start, then switched over to tractor fuel for normal running. The fuel tank has 2 chambers, one holding 10 gallons of gas and the other holding something like 90 gallons of fuel.

He and Ray Barrow began restoring it, first by removing the engine and taking it apart. They gave it a new set of piston rings, and took the 4 heads to a machine shop for reworking, which included magnafluxing to ensure they had no cracks, and grinding the valves and valve seats.

Checking the crank shaft and finding it perfect, they put the engine back together and reinstalled it. After putting gas and fuel in their respective tanks, they charged the priming cup with a tablespoon of gas and turned the engine over to suck the fluid into the cylinders.

The second time they pulled the engine over, it fired off and ran as beautifully as it did the day it rolled off the assembly line at the C. L. Best Tractor Co. plant of San Leandro, California, in 1925.

Bringing the newly restored old engine back to life marked the end of a process spanning about 11 years from the time he and Bill Santos found the tractor in California to that moment in Jimmy's shop.

It is easily the most attractive and awesome machine in Jimmy's collection, and the most valuable as well. He knows that because an executive of the Caterpillar Company who came to see the collection some years ago offered him somewhere in the neighborhood of a quarter of a million dollars for it, which, of course, he graciously declined.

No. 2 (p. 231), is a 1921 C. L. Best 30 Logging Cruiser, Serial Number S3656. It is a top-seat model, with a fold-down "buggy" top. The fold-down feature is to prevent damage to the top when working in heavily wooded areas where low hanging branches might bang it up.

Other features include a rear-mounted PTO designed for installation of a winch, or other PTO driven device. A fender cut-out gives a clear view of the serial plate, and it is "All-Fuel" designated, meaning it runs on either gasoline, tractor fuel, or other petroleum distillates.

In designing this tractor, the company copied the highly popular Best 60, but made it only half as big. The 30's popularity led the company to produce large numbers of them, especially the agricultural models. The logging cruisers however, enjoyed much less demand, resulting in fewer of them produced.

It is extremely rare and Jimmy believes no other exists that has been more faithfully restored to its original condition as a true top-seat logging cruiser. He thinks it is valued at about half that of the Best 60.

He found the tractor while searching along the back roads of Patterson, California. It sat in the front yard of a house he saw along the way. Recognizing it as a Best, he stopped to look at it.

When a woman answered his knock on the door, he expressed his interest in the tractor and wondered if she wanted to sell it. "Yes," she told him and when he asked how much, she told him 25 hundred dollars.

Following that came a man's voice from inside the house asking "Woman, what are you selling?" The woman told him to keep quiet back there. Hearing the man's footsteps approaching the door, Jimmy feared he might override the woman and cancel the deal.

Seeming to ignore the man, the woman told him she had just sold the tractor. The man shouted back; "Hell no, you can't sell it!"

Not wanting to get caught in the middle of a squabble between the two, Jimmy decided to make his exit. He told them if they wanted to sell the tractor for 25 hundred to please call him, after which he handed them his card and left.

About 2 months later, the man called Jimmy at home and told him he would sell the tractor for 3 thousand dollars. Knowing its value to be at least 6 thousand, Jimmy accepted the offer. After getting it transported to his farm, Jimmy and Ray Barrow restored it.

The buggy top, which came standard with that model of Best 30, had gone missing when Jimmy bought it. Tops built specifically for the tractor were no longer available, but Jimmy found a replacement at a Model T Ford parts factory in New York.

They could not however, provide him with anything closer to the original than one for a 1927 Model T roadster. Jimmy did not see that as a problem though. When he and Ray finished mounting it on the tractor, it looked as authentic and operated as well as the original with one exception; it had a rectangular rear widow, whereas the original had an oval shaped one.

No. 3 (p. 232), is a 1923 Holt Ten Ton Top Seat Logger. This gas-powered crawler features a rear mounted belt pulley, original special cast fuel tank cap, a rare military style spring wound starter, a rare military style pintle front towing hook, a right-hand drive position and original grouser bars added to the tracks in 2021.

The replaceable grouser bars facilitate changing them out to meet the traction demands of any given terrain. They came in a variety of sizes and shapes. Some were designed to increase flotation on soft ground, while others gave more aggressive traction on hard ground and rocky surfaces such as stone quarries. Those Jimmy installed in 2021 are designed for moderate traction needs.

As a second surface adapting feature, the Holt Ten Ton is the only crawler with a flexible track frame designed to maximize track contact with the surface on uneven terrain.

The downside of the system is that in flexed positions, the frame becomes shortened. That reduces the tension required to retain the tracks in place, subjecting them to separation from the frame in sharp turns.

The track separation problem far outweighed the flexing frame's surface contact advantage, leading to its demise in later crawler tractor undercarriages which favored nonflexible frames.

Jimmy acquired the tractor at an auction in Limon, Colorado, about 75 miles east of Denver. It belonged to a collector named Red Getty whose family put his estate up for auction after his death.

Jimmy, his former wife, Liz, and their friends, Darrell Harp and his wife, flew out to Colorado specifically for Jimmy to buy the tractor. The bidding began at 5 thousand and continued until Jimmy submitted the final bid of 10 thousand.

Harp, of Red Bay, Alabama, manufactured agricultural equipment and other products, many of which he trucked to the west coast. Jimmy hired him to haul the Holt from Colorado back to his farm on the return leg of one of his west coast runs.

Jimmy acquired the tractor sometime between 2000 and 2016 and he and Ray Barrow restored it during that same time period. Due to its unusual features and the small number of them remaining, the tractor is very rare.

No. 4 (p. 232), is a 1929 Caterpillar 60 Gas to Diesel Conversion crawler. The conversion involved an aftermarket arrangement wherein owners of Caterpillar 60 gas burners desiring diesel engines for their tractors purchased the new engines and had a dealer swap them out with the original.

The color scheme depicted in the photo reflects the change in colors the company adopted on 10 December 1931. Prior to that date, Caterpillar crawlers left the factory wearing coats of battle ship gray. After that date, they came out in sunny highway yellow.

The colors in the above photo indicate a tractor manufacture date prior to the color change and an engine manufacture date after the change. Jimmy believes that only about 4 of these conversions exist, but concedes there could be others he is unaware of. Regardless, the number remains so few as to make them extremely rare. The engine is 1 of only 56 made.

Another rare feature is the Caterpillar name printed on the inside back of the seat. It is the creation of John Hahn, owner of Hahn Tractor Seats, Craigmont, Idaho. As a custom feature on this tractor not found on most others, it is a "special seat." Lights and a front tow hook, are additional rare features of the tractor.

Jimmy bought it from Tom Madden of Paso Robles, California on the Pacific coast. He and Ray Barrow restored it.

No. 5 (p. 232), is a 1935 Caterpillar diesel 75 logger. The number of diesel 75s manufactured totaled approximately 875, but only about 1% were loggers, making them rare. Caterpillar introduced it as their first 6-cylinder diesel.

An onboard 2 cylinder "pony motor" with a 2-speed transmission starts the main engine. It has double seats; one for the driver during movement of the tractor and the other he uses when operating the winch. The winch is a 100-ton Hyster model with 2 reels; each with a cable length allowing for long-distance retrieval of logs in mountainous terrain. The tractor transmission is a slide shifter with 6 forwards and 2 reverses. A heavy steel towing hook is mounted on the frame beneath the radiator, which along with other related features, qualify it as a fully equipped logger.

The engine weighs 10 thousand pounds and the overall tractor weight is over 32 thousand pounds. Its coolant capacity is 38 gallons. Those familiar with the tractor consider to be the father of the later Caterpillar D-8.

Although he doesn't recall for certain, Jimmy thinks it probably came from the Spokane, Washington area. He and Ray Barrow restored it.

No. 6 (p. 232), is a 1934 Caterpillar 70 with the largest gas burning engine the company ever built. It is very rare due to only about 278 of them produced. It has an 8-speed transmission, consisting of 6 forwards and 2 reverses. Its overall weight is 31 thousand pounds.

Jimmy acquired it from Jim Zimmerman, a collector in Orchard, Iowa. He and Ray Barrow restored it.

No. 7 (p. 232), is a 1931 Caterpillar 65 gas crawler with a radiator whose rounded edges are a departure from those of the company's traditional angular design. Being the only model with that radiator in the company's history makes this tractor one of a kind.

Also unusual are the vented engine compartment side panels which were optional on Caterpillar tractors. The small number of 521 of them made, as documented by company literature, further contributes to its collectability rating as very rare. Intended as the replacement for the Caterpillar 60 with its battle ship grey color, on 10 December 1931, the company introduced this tractor as its first highway yellow model.

Jimmy acquired the tractor from Keith Clark of Spokane, Washington. He and Ray Barrow restored it.

No. 8 (p. 232), is a 1936 Caterpillar 30 WSP (Wide gage, Special). Wide-gage refers to the space between the tracks which give them a broader stance than standard gage models.

The purpose of the extra-wide undercarriage is to provide greater stability against overturning when driving laterally along steep slopes. It is a gas-powered version of wide gage models, which makes those that survive rare.

It is the last model to display the label, "Thirty," on front of the radiator. Equipped with a 5-speed transmission, it has electric start, "V" belt pulley and an hour meter.

The top corners of the seat back are cropped to give the operator an unobstructed view of implements in tow. The tractor is designated as "All-Fuel," meaning it runs on a variety of petroleum-based fuels, including gas, kerosene, tractor fuel and other distillates.

It was the tractor belonging to Mr. X which Jimmy confiscated from Orchard, Iowa, about 1999. He and Ray Barrow restored it.

No. 9 (p. 233), is a 1936 Caterpillar 40W (Wide gage) diesel crawler. It has a front tow hook, and onboard pony motor for starting the main engine. Approximately 2 thousand were built. It is rare due to the wide-gage undercarriage.

Jimmy found it in California about 2003 and he and Ray Barrow restored it.

No. 10 (233), is a 1935 Caterpillar PCG (Power Controlled Grader). The power-controlled feature refers to an onboard 5 hp single cylinder Caterpillar built engine which powered all the machine's functions, including power steering, wheel leaning, wheel offset and crabbing.

The Company often quipped about it being the smallest engine Caterpillar ever built. Jimmy found it sitting in a field near Tulare, California. He bought it from the owner for 1 thousand dollars, and paid 15 hundred to get it trucked to Florida. Jimmy and Charles Kinky restored it.

It ended the Company's tow-behind grader production. All graders following it were self-propelled motor graders.

No. 11 (p. 233) is a 1931 Caterpillar 25W (Wide-gage) gas crawler. A rare early production model, it came off the assembly line as the 83rd of approximately 3 hundred built. Its serial number is 3C83, with the last 2 digits corresponding to its sequence in production.

It was based on a 1927 Caterpillar 20 design that evolved into a 25, following modifications to improve its performance in 1931.

It features vented engine compartment side panels and a double drawbar with high and low positions. The color scheme is an example of the factory paint job prior to the change-over to highway yellow.

Jimmy acquired it in a trade for a rare 9900 Caterpillar engine he found at a defunct sawmill on Lincton Mountain near the cabin he built in Oregon. He and Ray Barrow restored it.

Although Jimmy has restored dozens of tractors, he bought and sold many more that he did not restore. When he sells a tractor, he prefers that it go to someone who shares his interest in giving life to the old machine and will treat it like he would himself.

At times, a little charity may have gone along with a sale if Jimmy liked the man buying it. That happened with an old Caterpillar he sold a friend in Panama City a few years back. Jimmy knew him to be a nice guy and a good mechanic and that he would lovingly restore the tractor to like new condition.

The old tractor had been sitting under one of his sheds for about 12 years when the man approached him about buying it. Jimmy sold it to him for what he had in it and the man took it home to Panama City and restored it.

Hard times befell him when Hurricane Michael devastated his property on October 10, 2018. It destroyed every building standing on his 5 acres, and he had to rebuild it all. In the midst of that, his best friend got fired from his job and he was trying to help him out while rebuilding his own property. On top of everything else, his wife became un-happy with the way things were going, and she left.

On the verge of desperation, he paid Jimmy a visit and told him he had so many problems that he needed to sell the tractor because of all the money he had in it and he needed the money more than he needed the tractor.

Jimmy considered him a good friend and wanted to help him if he could. He told him to go get his wife back, work things out with her and get their lives back in order. Then bring his tractor back and he would help him sell it.

The guy said OK and left. Six months later he had his wife back and other problems worked out except he still needed to sell the tractor to help with his money problems.

He brought the tractor back to Jimmy and said he had put 7 thousand into it, with the purchase price and cost of everything he had done to it. But because he needed the money, he would let it go for 6 thousand.

Jimmy told him that rather than trying to sell it for him, which might take longer than he could afford to wait, he would just buy it from him for 6 thousand on the spot. The man told him he appreciated that, because it would help him out when he needed it the most.

Jimmy gave him a check for the amount and he left happier than when he arrived. Four days later, a man visiting the farm saw the tractor and loved it. He asked Jimmy what he wanted for it and Jimmy told him; 7 thousand.

He bought it, Jimmy loaded it on his trailer and he left. Two hours later, he called Jimmy and thanked him for selling him the tractor. He loved it; he said. It was just what he wanted.

Jimmy got on the phone with his friend in Panama City he bought the tractor from and told him he just sold it for 7 thousand dollars. He told him that since he had more in it than the 6 thousand he paid him, he would give him the other thousand so that he got out of it everything he had put into it.

"You can't do that," the friend told him, "You bought it, it was yours and the profit is yours." "No," Jimmy told him, "You need the money worse than I do. I gave you 6 thousand for it as a favor, and this is just another favor, and I want you to have it. I won't take no for an answer."

"I cannot imagine you doing this," the friend told him, "But I am grateful that you are."

And that, Jimmy said, is spirituality. It is what God intended for us to do for our brothers and sisters in whatever way we can or should.

"I don't give to organized charities, like Red Cross and United Way, etc. But I give it personally to people like him that I know needs it," he said. He had done a lot of that over the years, he declared, and it always worked well.

VIII

≈EPILOGUE≈

A Museum for Jimmy's Tractor Collection, His Plans for the Future and Biographical Sketches of his Children.

When looking back on the decisions he made in the past, Jimmy believes that at every turning point he faced, or every challenge he confronted, he chose the best path forward as he saw it at the time.

At the age of 87, he remains unapologetic in that belief and holds to it as the guiding principle in his

Dr. Jimmy Sheppard. Photo by Sam Carnley, 2021.

life. Once he made a decision, he fully dedicated himself to accomplishing the objective on which he set his sights.

To put it simply, he made the choices he did because in his mind, "it was the right thing to do." The good deeds he has done and continues to do, and the successes he has enjoyed, tend to affirm the validity of that belief.

The splendid restored antique tractor collection he amassed confirms that his decision to restore tractors those many years ago, "was the right thing to do."

He began the hobby because he enjoyed it and continues doing it for the same reason. He believes at this stage of his life it remains the right thing to do and plans to keep doing it as long as he is able.

The Walton County Board of Commissioners recently approached him about establishing a museum to house his antique tractors to which he agreed. He offered a donation of 3 million dollars in support of the project.

Consideration of the museum by the county is ongoing as of this writing and whether it will become a reality cannot be predicted.

In the event the museum does not come to fruition, he has made no other plans for the final disposition of the collection. Prior to Martha's death, he deeded his rights in their property to her.

She then prepared a will distributing the property to their 4 children and giving Jimmy a life-time estate in their home. Execution of the will took place following her death in 1997. He will leave what happens to the tractors up to whomever inherits them at his death.

But thoughts of his demise rarely cross his mind. He focuses more on living and remembering how good life has been to him. A powerful reminder of that came in 2020 with an invitation to celebrate with cherished acquaintances from the past.

His friends and benefactors from his pre-med school days, Norm and Helene Hibbard, then 90 years old, had been together for 7 decades. They sent him an invitation to join them in celebrating their 70th wedding anniversary on July 28 at their home in Tuscaloosa, which he of course, attended.

He last visited his cabin near Pendleton, Oregon in October, 2021. Penny accompanied him and plans to make the cabin her new home. He changed his deed to the property making her a co-owner and ultimately, she will become the sole owner.

Penny is an accountant, and is involved in 2 business enterprises. One is the hunting and fishing guide service on the Quinault Indian reservation near Amanda Park in Washington State.

The other is a new camp ground project she is involved in developing near the cabin in Oregon. It will be an 80-acre complex including cabins, a restaurant and service station.

Pam, Jimmy's second daughter, lives in the house on Bruce Creek farm her family moved into when they first came there in 1974. She received the house and 25 acres of land in her mother's will. She is single and has no children.

She is now employed by the Best Western Motel in DeFuniak Springs as a general maintenance worker.

Polly, the 3rd in order of birth of the "3 Ps," as her parents called her and her 2 sisters when they were children, lives in Oregon and has worked for more than 30 years as a senior flight attendant for Delta Airlines. She is married to Emilio Biasucci, of Italian and Spanish descent. She speaks fluent Italian, which has benefitted her tremendously in her career. They have no children.

Ballard was the last child born to Martha and Jimmy. He received a degree in education and taught school for a time but soon found it not to his liking.

His wife, Sarah, who had also gone into education, felt the same way. Paying Jimmy a visit, they told him how unhappy they were in their jobs and that they would like to go back to college and try something else.

He gave them his blessing and the financial support to the extent they needed it. Ballard went back and earned a PHD in clinical psychology. He is a licensed clinical counselor and serves as CEO of the hospital in Birmingham where he is employed. He has held the position since 2019.

Sarah became a dentist and heads her own clinic, also in Birmingham. They have a small son. His name is Barrett.

Jimmy's brother and parents (L to R) Arthur Robert, Arthur and Lola Sheppard, Ca 1960, at home in Rehobeth, Alabama. Photo courtesy of Penny Sheppard Jordan.

The wedding of Jimmy Sheppard and Martha Claire McGilvray, 30 May 1959, in Birmingham, Alabama. Photo courtesy of Penny Sheppard Jordan.

The Sheppards, (L to R), Martha, Penny and Jimmy (M. D., captain, USAF), Eglin AFB, Florida, about 1962. Photo courtesy of Penny Sheppard Jordan.

Dr. Jimmy and Martha Sheppard, Christmas 1996, just 16 days before Martha died, January 10, 1997. Photo courtesy of Penny Sheppard Jordan.

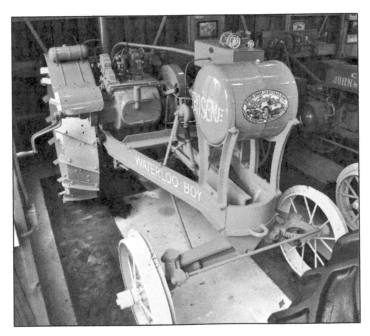

No. 1, view A

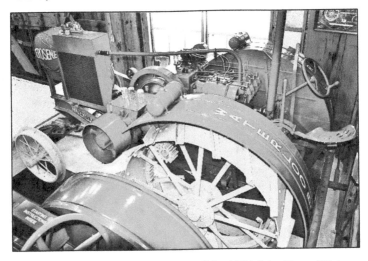

No. 1, view B. These 2 views are of the 1924 John Deere Waterloo Boy N in Jimmy's collection. See narrative No 1, p. 178.

No. 2. 1924 John Deere D, aka the "Spoker" D. See No. 2 narrative, p. 180.

No. 3. 1932 John Deere GPO (General Purpose, Orchard). See No. 3 narrative, p. 183.

No. 4. 1933 John Deere GP, (General Purpose), See No. 4 narrative, p. 184.

No. 5. 1934 John Deere A, Dural Rear Wheels. See No. 5 narrative, p. 185.

No. 6. 1935 John Deere Garden
B. See No. 6 narrative, p. 185.

No. 7. 1937 John Deere AOS (A, Orchard, Streamlined).
See No. 7 narrative, p. 186.

No. 8. 1938 John Deere AWH (A, Wide, High). See No. 8 narrative, p. 187.

No. 9. 1938 John Deere BI (B, Industrial). See No. 9 narrative, p. 187.

No. 10. 1938 John Deere G-Big Radiator, Dual Rear Wheels. See No. 10 narrative, p. 189.

No. 11. 1938 John Deere G-Low Radiator. See No. 11 narrative, p. 190.

No. 12. 1950 John Deere MTW (MT, Wide). See No. 12 narrative, p. 191.

No. 13. 1942 John Deere H. See No. 13 narrative, p. 192.

No. 14. 1959 John Deere 830I (Industrial). See No. 14 narrative, p. 193.

No. 15. 1959-60 John Deere 840I (Industrial). See No. 15 narrative p. 193.

No. 1. 1925 C. L. Best 60 Logging Cruiser. See No. 1 narrative, p. 201.

No. 2. 1921 C. L. Best 30 Logging Cruiser. See No. 2 narrative, p. 206.

No. 3. 1923 Holt 10 Ton Top Seat Logger. See No. 3 narrative, p. 208.

No. 4. 1929 Caterpillar Gas-to Diesel Conversion. See No. 4 narrative, p. 209.

No. 5. 1935 Caterpillar Diesel 75 Logger. See No. 5 narrative, p. 210.

No. 6. 1934 Caterpillar 70 Gas Crawler. See No. 6 narrative, p. 211.

No. 7. 1931 Caterpillar 65 Gas Crawler. See No. 7 narrative, p. 211.

No. 8. 1936 Caterpillar 30WSP, All-Fuel Crawler. See No. 8 narrative, p. 212.

No. 10. 1935 Caterpillar PCG (Power Controlled Grader). See No. 10 narrative, p. 213.

No. 9. 1936 Caterpillar 40W Diesel Crawler. See No. 9 narrative, p. 213.

No. 11. **(Right)** 1931 Caterpillar 25W Crawler. See No. 11 narrative, p. 213.

(Left) Jimmy and Penny's cabin in Oregon. Photo taken by Penny in the winter of 2021-2022 after snow had fallen.

Penny Sheppard Jordan.

Pam Sheppard

Emilio and Polly Sheppard Biasucci
Photo courtesy of Penny S. Jordan.

Ballard Sheppard.

(**L to R**) Dr. Robert Sheppard, Lola Frances Sheppard Parish
and Dr. Jimmy Sheppard; siblings. Photo Courtesy of Frances.

BIBLIOGRAPHY

Rural Electrification Administration (REA)
https://livingnewdeal.org/glossary/rural-electrifica-tion-administration-rea-1935/

Hutchinson, Daniel,
World War II POW Camps in Alabama,
Florida State University,
Published: January 7, 2008 | Last updated: November 7, 2013
http://www.encyclopediaofalabama.org/article/h-1418

Drake, Sarah,
Windmill Station used as POW camp for German soldiers in WWII
Posted: Jun 6, 2019 / 11:29 PM CDT / Updated: Jun 6, 2019 / 11:29 PM CDT
DOTHAN, Ala. (WDHN)
https://www.dothanfirst.com/news/windmill-station-used-as-pow-camp-for-german-soldiers-in-wwii/2058931681/

Collingham, Lizzie, THE TASTE OF WAR,
How World War II Changed The Way Americans Ate,
Commercial bakeries given preference in sugar rationing
Reprinted by arrangement with The Penguin Press, a member of Penguin Group (USA), Inc. Copyright (c) Lizzie Collingham, 2012.
https://www.huffpost.com/entry/wwii-food-america_n_1398132

Schumm, Laura,
Food Rationing in Wartime America,
Sugar rationing continued until 1947
Updated: aug 31, 2018
Original: may 23, 2014
https://www.history.com/news/food-rationing-in-wartime-america

SUGAR
"U. S. consumers register for first ration books". Life. 11 May 1942. p. 19. Retrieved 17 November 2011.
https://books.google.com/books?id=CVAEAAAAM-BAJ&lpg=PA19&pg=PA22#v=onepage&q&f=true

Sundin, Sarah,
> Make It Do – Sugar Rationing in World War II
> *POSTED: Monday, January 31, 2011 by*
> https://www.sarahsundin.com/make-it-do-sugar-rationing-in-world-war-ii-2/

The Henry Ford,
> The Vagabonds
> https://www.thehenryford.org/collections-and-research/digital-resources/popular-topics/the-vagabonds/

Thomas Edison's Florida,
> The New York Times
> https://www.nytimes.com/1990/06/24/travel/thomas-edison-s-florida.html

Tripler Army Medical Center,
> Wikipedia
> https://en.wikipedia.org/wiki/Tripler_Army_Medical_Center

Eglin AFB,
> Wikipedia
> https://en.wikipedia.org/wiki/Eglin_Air_Force_Base

Striepe, Becky'
> Who invented sports drinks?
> https://science.howstuffworks.com/innovation/everyday-innovations/who-invented-sports-drinks.htm/printable

Robert Cade,
> Wikipedia
> https://en.wikipedia.org/wiki/Robert_Cade

Ray Graves,
> Wikipedia
> https://en.wikipedia.org/wiki/Ray_Graves

Gatorade,
> Wikipedia
> https://en.wikipedia.org/wiki/Gatorade

Dana Shires,
> Wikipedia
> https://en.wikipedia.org/wiki/Dana_Shires

Dr. James Robert Cade- Gatorade inventor
> UF History of Medicine, College of Medicine
> https://history.med.ufl.edu/profiles-in-history/dr-robert-cade/

Gordon, Mark,
> Thirst Quencher – Dr. Alejandro de Quesada
> Business Observer, January 17, 2014
> https://www.businessobserverfl.com/article/thirst-quencher

Tractor Data.com

    John Deere Farm Tractors by Model

    https://www.tractordata.com/farm-tractors/tractor-brands/johndeere/johndeere-tractors.html

Antique Caterpillar Machinery Owner's Club (ACMOC)

    Caterpillar History

    https://www.acmoc.org/about/cat-history

Benjamín Holt

    Wikipedia

    https://en.wikipedia.org/wiki/Benjamin_Holt

Holt Manufacturing Company

    Wikipedia

    https://en.wikipedia.org/wiki/Holt_Manufacturing_Company

Daniel Best

    Wikipedia

    https://en.wikipedia.org/wiki/Daniel_Best

Best Manufacturing Company

    Wikipedia

    https://en.wikipedia.org/wiki/Best_Manufacturing_Company

Caterpillar, Inc.

    Wikipedia

    https://en.wikipedia.org/wiki/Caterpillar_Inc.

The 840

    Johnnypopper.com

    http://johnnypopper.com/weirddeere/The_840.html

Yellowhouse Machinery

    https://yhmc.com/About-Us.aspx

C. L. Best

    Wikipedia

    https://en.wikipedia.org/wiki/C._L._Best

Orlemann, Eric,

    Caterpillar Chronicle, (MBI Publishing Company,729 Prospect Ave. PO Box 1, Osceola, WI 54020-0001, USA)

ABOUT THE AUTHOR

Sam Carnley, at age 79 is a fledgling author looking forward to his first award winning credits. He earned a bachelor's degree in accounting from the University of West Florida, class of 1976. He retired in 2010 from a more than 30-year career as an accountant, auditor and chief financial officer. He loves history, especially about his home county of Walton. As a member of the Walton County Heritage Association, Inc. of DeFuniak Springs, Florida, since 2013, he writes and publishes online the Association's monthly newsletter, "Walton Relations & History." It contains primarily articles of historical interest about the county. This biography is his first venture into book writing and he hopes only the first of many more to come.